SWEET, SAVORY + SOMETIMES BOOZY CUPCAKES

ALISON RIEDE
Photos by **MOLLY HAUGE**

SWEET, SAVORY*
CUPCAKES

THE COUNTRYMAN PRESS · WOODSTOCK, VT.

* AND SOMETIMES BOOZY

Published by The Countryman Press,
P.O. Box 748, Woodstock, VT 05091
Distributed by W. W. Norton & Company, Inc.,
500 Fifth Avenue, New York, NY 10110

Printed in China
Designed by Natalie Olsen, Kisscut Design

Sweet, Savory, and Sometimes Boozy Cupcakes

978-1-58157-297-1

10 9 8 7 6 5 4 3 2 1

"A party without cake is just a meeting."
—JULIA CHILD

CONTENTS

FOREWORD

"This is what Cupcake Wars *is all about."*

Those were the first words I said to Alison Riede after I tasted her Sharp Cheddar Cupcake with Honey Blue Cheese Frosting and Candied Pecan Topping. It was Season 4 of *Cupcake Wars* and I had tasted my fair share of unusual flavor combinations over the previous three seasons. The first round of each episode of *Cupcake Wars* is always based 100 percent on taste, and taste alone, so we challenge bakers to create a delicious cupcake using ingredients not commonly found in a cupcake. Typically those ingredients contain savory elements normally reserved for cooking, not baking. Alison was a contestant on a holiday episode, based on the Hollywood Christmas Parade event, so she was challenged to create a cupcake using an old-fashioned, outdated Christmas dish. Her options included string bean casserole, oyster pudding, fruitcake, and a cheese log. She chose the latter, and I was instantly impressed by her ability to balance the savory, sharp Cheddar with the nutty, strong flavor of the blue cheese in the frosting while keeping some sweetness with a touch of honey and the toasted candied pecans.

While growing up in Paris, I knew at an early age I wanted to get into baking and pastry arts as a career. I've been working in professional kitchens in Paris and the United States since 1983, and it's interesting to watch the way trends in the culinary industry come and go. Cupcakes have been a huge, growing trend for the last ten years. In 2005 Candace Nelson opened Sprinkles Cupcakes, which is considered the first bakery specializing in cupcakes alone. Since then, cupcakes have stopped taking a back seat to traditional cakes and are becoming the main dessert at many weddings, birthday parties, and large events. Cupcakes can now be considered a sophisticated dessert worthy of a black-tie event. Not all that long ago it seemed that if you wanted to bake your own cupcakes you had to buy a box mix at the grocery store, with three flavors to choose from: vanilla, chocolate, and red velvet. Now there are countless gourmet options available, such as pistachio, salted caramel, and flourless chocolate. With the emergence of this new cupcake trend came a new competition of cupcake bakers, each eager to outdo the other and take cupcakes to the next level.

Cupcake Wars, which first aired in 2010, has challenged bakers to think outside the box and take more risks. In order to win an episode of *Cupcake Wars*, you have to be willing to experiment with savory ingredients such as fried chicken, avocados, and black beans while still making your cupcake taste delicious. It's rare that bakers can strike this balance between sweet and savory, but I believe this is the way the cupcake industry is headed. Alison has told me that her experience on *Cupcake Wars* changed her thinking on cupcakes forever; now she's constantly finding inspiration for new cupcake recipes, whether it's tasting an ethnic dish for the first time, wine tasting, or trying out a new cocktail at a restaurant.

Sweet, Savory, and Sometimes Boozy Cupcakes is a cookbook for creative and modern bakers, amateur or experienced, who want to impress their friends with something new, something avant-garde. There are cupcake recipes featuring an array of cheeses, such as camembert and parmesan, and fresh herbs and spices, such as rosemary, sage, and herbes de Provence. My personal favorite, the Sharp Cheddar Cupcake, also makes an appearance. These are the perfect cupcakes to entertain with; they'll give your guests a conversation topic, and you'll have an excuse to open a bottle of wine to pair with them.

Bon appetit!

Florian Bellanger

Executive Pastry Chef, Founder and Co-Owner of Mad Mac NYC. Permanent Judge on the Food Network's "Cupcake Wars"

INTRODUCTION

As I quickly discovered when I competed on the show — and won — *Cupcake Wars*, the world of cupcake flavors has moved well beyond vanilla with rainbow sprinkles! The cupcake world is heading in another, more mature direction: savory and sometimes boozy cupcakes.

Many people are thrown off when they hear some of my cupcake flavors, such as Sharp Cheddar, Rosemary Parmesan, and even Chicken 'n' Waffle. Being on *Cupcake Wars* forced me to think outside the box, because I had to find a way to stand apart and win. I've started using different herbs, cheeses, wines, beers, and even vegetables in my cupcakes. My Cucumber Mint Cupcake is one of my absolute favorites; it's refreshing, light, and has a subtle sweetness.

I have personally experienced the flavor evolution of cupcakes, from cupcakes being very cutesy and girly, to becoming more sophisticated and elevated. In fact, I've started pairing my cupcakes with wine at a local tasting room called Corks n' Crowns in Santa Barbara, and the response has been incredible. It's been a perfect testing ground for new cupcake recipes, and I've discovered that people are curious to try unlikely flavors, partly to say they've tried them!

I don't know about you, but if something is new and exclusive, I want to try it. That's why I like to experiment with savory flavors, not only are they unexpected, but they are surprisingly delicious. Some people will say they aren't "dessert people," but the combination of lightly sweet and savory flavors will open their minds to the idea of dessert. I was inspired to create this cookbook that strikes the balance of sweet and savory, and make these recipes accessible to everyone.

SWEE
SAVO
CUPC

T, RY* AKES

1
TART + CITRUSY + LIGHT

2
Pink Champagne
Cupcake
+ Vanilla
Champagne
Buttercream

6
Lemon Olive Oil
Cupcake
+ Sage Frosting

8
Earl Grey
Cupcake
+ Earl Grey
Lemon Zest
Buttercream

11
Mimosa
Cheesecake
Cupcake
+ Orange
Champagne
Frosting

14
Margarita
Cupcake
+ Tequila Lime
Buttercream

16
Rosewater
Cupcake
+ Rosewater
Lemon
Buttercream

20
Orange
Chardonnay
Cupcake
+ Orange
Mascarpone
Frosting

22
White Chocolate
Coconut Cupcake
+ White
Chocolate Lime
Buttercream

26
Elderflower
Cupcake
+ Lemon Zest
Buttercream

PINK
CHAMPAGNE
CUPCAKE
+VANILLA
CHAMPAGNE
BUTTERCREAM

I baked these cupcakes for my best friend's (and Cupcake Wars partner) wedding. She's always loved the light, fluffy taste of these cupcakes, and there's always something celebratory about popping open a bottle of champagne! It's truly the perfect wedding cupcake.

PINK CHAMPAGNE CUPCAKE

1 cup granulated sugar

¾ cup butter, softened

2 eggs

1 teaspoon pure vanilla extract

½ cup dry champagne

¼ cup sour cream

¾ cup all-purpose flour

½ cup self-rising flour

½ teaspoon baking soda

¼ teaspoon salt

5–7 drops red food coloring
(or until desired color)

TOTAL TIME

60
minutes

15
CUPCAKES

Preheat the oven to 350°F. Line two standard cupcake tins with 15 paper liners.

Using a stand or hand mixer, cream together the sugar and butter on medium speed in a large bowl.

Slowly add in eggs, one at a time, and mix on medium speed until combined.

Reduce speed to low and add vanilla extract, champagne, and sour cream.

In a separate bowl, combine both flours, baking soda, and salt. Slowly add dry ingredients to wet ingredients, and mix on medium speed until smooth, about 1 minute.

Slowly add in red food coloring until the batter turns the desired shade of pink.

Using a large spoon, fill the cupcake liners three-quarters full and bake for 18 to 20 minutes, or until a toothpick inserted in the center comes out clean. Let cool for 20 minutes.

VANILLA CHAMPAGNE BUTTERCREAM

½ cup butter, softened
1 teaspoon pure vanilla extract
¼ cup dry champagne
3 cups powdered sugar
Pink sugar, for garnish

With a hand or stand mixer, beat softened butter and vanilla extract together on medium speed for 2 minutes.

Slowly add half of the dry champagne, and then add 1 cup of the powdered sugar and beat on low for 1 minute.

Slowly add the remaining champagne and powdered sugar alternately until everything is combined.

Gradually increase the speed to high and beat for 3 minutes, until fluffy.

To Assemble Cupcakes
Gently pipe each cupcake with Vanilla Champagne Buttercream. Garnish with pink sugar.

LEMON OLIVE OIL CUPCAKE + SAGE FROSTING

This is my go-to cupcake for entertaining, because it basically appeals to everyone. It's sweet and salty, with a refreshing tartness from the lemon. The olive oil keeps the cake incredibly moist, and the unexpected addition of sage creates a unique depth of flavor. Be prepared for lots of people to ask for the recipe at the end of the night!

LEMON OLIVE OIL CUPCAKE

2 eggs
1 cup granulated sugar
4 teaspoons pure lemon extract
¼ cup whole milk
½ cup sour cream
¾ cup all-purpose flour
½ cup self-rising flour
½ teaspoon baking soda
¼ teaspoon salt
1 cup olive oil

Preheat the oven to 350°F. Line two standard cupcake tins with 15 paper liners.

Using a stand or hand mixer, cream together the eggs and sugar on medium speed in a large bowl.

Reduce speed to low and add lemon extract, milk, and sour cream.

In a separate bowl, combine both flours, baking soda, and salt. Slowly add dry ingredients to wet ingredients, and mix on medium speed until smooth, about 1 minute.

Slowly add olive oil and mix on medium speed for 1 minute, or until combined.

Using a large spoon, fill the cupcake liners three-quarters full and bake for 18 to 20 minutes, or until a toothpick inserted in the center comes out clean. Let cool for 20 minutes.

SAGE FROSTING

1 cup butter, softened
½ cup cream cheese
2 cups powdered sugar
2½ teaspoons ground sage
Sea salt, to taste, for garnish

With a hand or stand mixer, beat
softened butter and cream cheese
together on medium speed for
3 minutes.

Slowly add powdered sugar and beat
on low for 1 minute.

Add ground sage and gradually
increase the speed to high and beat
for 3 minutes, until fluffy.

To Assemble Cupcakes
Gently pipe each cupcake with Sage
Frosting. Garnish with a sprinkle of
sea salt on each cupcake.

EARL GREY CUPCAKE + EARL GREY LEMON ZEST BUTTERCREAM

When I lived in Brooklyn, there was a tea and coffee shop at the end of my block called The Tea Lounge. I would stop in there almost every day before I took the F train into Manhattan. The shop had hundreds of different types of tea, but I almost always got a cup of Earl Grey. Unfortunately, The Tea Lounge has since closed, so this cupcake is my tribute to it. Earl Grey Infused Milk is a key ingredient in these delicious cupcakes.

EARL GREY CUPCAKE

1 cup granulated sugar
¾ cup butter, softened
2 eggs
1 teaspoon pure vanilla extract
½ cup Earl Grey Infused Milk (recipe follows)
¼ cup sour cream
¾ cup all-purpose flour
½ cup self-rising flour
½ teaspoons baking soda
½ teaspoon salt

Preheat the oven to 350°F. Line two standard cupcake tins with 15 paper liners.

Using a stand or hand mixer, cream together the sugar and butter on medium speed in a large bowl.

Slowly add in eggs, one at a time, and mix on medium speed until combined.

Reduce speed to low and add vanilla extract, Earl Grey Infused Milk, and sour cream.

In a separate bowl, combine both flours, baking soda, and salt. Slowly add dry ingredients to wet ingredients, and mix on medium speed until smooth, about 2 minutes.

Using a large spoon, fill the cupcake liners three-quarters full and bake for 18 to 20 minutes, or until a toothpick inserted in the center comes out clean. Let cool for 20 minutes.

✳ *Make the Earl Grey Infused Milk first, and then make the cupcakes.*

EARL GREY LEMON ZEST BUTTERCREAM

1 cup butter, softened
1½ teaspoons lemon zest
¼ cup Earl Grey Infused Milk (recipe follows)
4 cups powdered sugar

With a hand or stand mixer, beat softened butter and lemon zest together on medium speed for 3 minutes.

Add Earl Grey Infused Milk and mix on medium speed until thoroughly combined.

Slowly add powdered sugar and beat on low for 1 minute.

Gradually increase the speed to high and beat for 3 minutes, until fluffy.

EARL GREY INFUSED MILK

5 bags of Earl Grey tea
1 cup whole milk

Heat 5 tea bags and 1 cup milk over high heat for 2 minutes, or until bubbles form.

Reduce heat to low and let simmer for 3 minutes, stirring constantly with a wooden spoon. Remove from heat and let stand for 15 minutes.

With your hands, squeeze the excess liquid from the tea bags and discard them. Save ½ cup for Earl Grey Cupcakes and ¼ cup for Earl Grey Lemon Zest Buttercream

To Assemble Cupcakes
Gently pipe each cupcake with Earl Grey Lemon Zest Buttercream.

MIMOSA
CHEESECAKE
CUPCAKE
+ORANGE
CHAMPAGNE
FROSTING

*Mimosa Cheesecake has
been one of my signature
flavors since I opened Sugar
Cat Studio. It's the perfect
"brunch" cupcake, because
after you've enjoyed your
eggs Benedict, or bacon
cheddar quiche, you'll want
a sweet treat for dessert.
Plus, it pairs perfectly with
that last mimosa you're
finishing.*

MIMOSA CHEESECAKE CUPCAKE

6 ounces vanilla wafers, about 35–40 wafers
¼ cup butter
24 ounces cream cheese
1 cup granulated sugar
2 large eggs
2 teaspoons pure orange extract

Preheat the oven to 325°F. Line a standard cupcake tin with 12 paper liners.

In a blender or food processor, pulse together the vanilla wafers until they resemble fine sand. Transfer wafer crumbs to a medium bowl and set aside.

In a separate, small bowl, melt butter in the microwave until it is completely liquid.

Pour butter into the vanilla wafer crumbs and mix well with a fork, until the mixture is thoroughly combined.

Press one rounded tablespoon of the wafer mixture into the bottom of each cupcake liner.

Using a stand or hand mixer on the lowest speed, beat together the cream cheese and sugar until smooth.

Beat in one egg at a time, increasing the speed to high after the last egg is added. Beat for about 3 minutes, until the batter is smooth.

Lowering the speed to low, add orange extract and mix for 30 seconds.

TOTAL TIME
70
minutes

TOTAL
TIME
70
minutes

Fill cupcake liners all the way to the top; they will hardly rise at all during baking.

Bake for 25 minutes, or until cheesecake starts to crack on the top, and the edges are slightly golden. Remove from oven and chill in the refrigerator for 20 minutes, or until firm. While cupcakes are chilling, prepare Orange Champagne Frosting.

ORANGE CHAMPAGNE FROSTING

½ cup butter, softened
1 teaspoon pure orange extract
4 tablespoons dry champagne
3 cups powdered sugar
Zest of one orange, for garnish

With a hand or stand mixer, beat softened butter and orange extract together on medium speed for 2 minutes.

Slowly add 2 tablespoons of the dry champagne, and then add 2 cups of the powdered sugar and beat on low for 1 minute. Add the remaining champagne and powdered sugar alternately until everything is combined.

Gradually increase the speed to high and beat for 3 minutes, until fluffy.

To Assemble Cupcakes
Gently pipe each cupcake with Orange Champagne Frosting. Garnish with a sprinkle of orange zest on each cupcake.

MARGARITA CUPCAKE ✛ TEQUILA LIME BUTTERCREAM

This is the definition of a party cupcake. I served these cupcakes on Cinco de Mayo one year, which is a holiday that people in Santa Barbara take very seriously. It's almost like taking a shot of tequila, in cupcake form. Keep this cupcake away from the kids!

MARGARITA CUPCAKE

1 cup granulated sugar
¾ cup butter, softened
2 eggs
½ cup lime juice
¼ cup sour cream
¾ cup all-purpose flour
½ cup self-rising flour
½ teaspoon baking soda
1 teaspoon baking powder
¼ teaspoon salt

Preheat the oven to 350°F. Line two standard cupcake tins with 15 paper liners.

Using a stand or hand mixer, cream together the sugar and butter on medium speed in a large bowl.

Slowly add in eggs, one at a time, and mix on medium speed until combined.

Reduce speed to low and add lime juice and sour cream.

In a separate bowl, combine both flours, baking soda, baking powder, and salt. Slowly add dry ingredients to wet ingredients, and mix on medium speed until smooth, about 1 minute.

Using a large spoon, fill the cupcake liners three-quarters full and bake for 18 to 20 minutes, or until a toothpick inserted in the center comes out clean. Let cool for 20 minutes.

TEQUILA LIME BUTTERCREAM

½ cup butter, softened
2 tablespoons tequila
¼ teaspoon salt
2 cups powdered sugar
Zest of 1 lime, for garnish
Sprinkle of sea salt, for garnish

With a hand or stand mixer, beat softened butter and tequila together on medium speed for 3 minutes.

Add salt and mix on medium speed until thoroughly combined.

Slowly add powdered sugar and beat on low for 1 minute.

Gradually increase the speed to high and beat for 3 minutes, until fluffy.

To Assemble Cupcakes
Gently pipe each cupcake with Tequila Lime Buttercream. Garnish with a sprinkle of lime zest and sea salt on each cupcake.

ROSEWATER CUPCAKE + ROSEWATER LEMON BUTTERCREAM

The first time I baked these cupcakes was for Mother's Day. I figured it would be the perfect present for my mom: flowers and cake all in one bite! I purchase edible flowers online, and I have them shipped overnight so they stay fresh.

ROSEWATER CUPCAKE

1 cup granulated sugar
¾ cup butter, softened
2 eggs
¼ cup rosewater
½ cup sour cream
¾ cup all-purpose flour
½ cup self-rising flour
½ teaspoon baking soda
¼ teaspoon salt

TOTAL TIME
60
minutes

Preheat the oven to 350°F. Line two standard cupcake tins with 15 paper liners.

Using a stand or hand mixer, cream together the sugar and butter on medium speed in a large bowl.

Slowly add eggs one at a time.

Reduce speed to low and add rosewater and sour cream.

In a separate bowl, combine both flours, baking soda, and salt. Slowly add dry ingredients to wet ingredients, and mix on medium speed until smooth, about 2 minutes.

Using a large spoon, fill the cupcake liners three-quarters full and bake for 18 to 20 minutes, or until a toothpick inserted in the center comes out clean. Let cool for 20 minutes.

ROSEWATER LEMON BUTTERCREAM

½ cup butter, softened
½ tablespoon rosewater
2 cups powdered sugar
½ tablespoon fresh squeezed lemon juice
Zest of one lemon, for garnish
12 edible roses, for garnish

With a hand or stand mixer, beat softened butter and rosewater together on medium speed for 3 minutes.

Slowly add powdered sugar and beat on low for 1 minute.

Add lemon juice and gradually increase the speed to high and beat for 3 minutes, until fluffy.

To Assemble Cupcakes
Gently pipe each cupcake with Rosewater Lemon Buttercream. Garnish with a sprinkle of fresh lemon zest and top each cupcake with an edible rose.

ORANGE CHARDONNAY CUPCAKE + ORANGE MASCARPONE FROSTING

Every Sunday I pair my cupcakes with sparkling wine at a wine tasting room called Corks n' Crowns in downtown Santa Barbara. This Orange Chardonnay Cupcake pairs exceptionally well with blanc de blancs (meaning white of whites), which is a sparkling wine most commonly made from chardonnay grapes. Bake a batch of these cupcakes for an excuse to pop open a bottle of bubbly!

ORANGE CHARDONNAY CUPCAKE

1 cup granulated sugar
¾ cup butter, softened
2 eggs
1 teaspoon pure orange extract
½ cup chardonnay
¼ cup sour cream
¾ cup all-purpose flour
½ cup self-rising flour
½ teaspoon baking soda
¼ teaspoon salt

Preheat the oven to 350°F. Line two standard cupcake tins with 15 paper liners.

Using a stand or hand mixer, cream together the sugar and butter on medium speed in a large bowl.

Slowly add in eggs, one at a time, and mix on medium speed until combined.

Reduce speed to low and add orange extract, chardonnay, and sour cream.

In a separate bowl, combine both flours, baking soda, and salt. Slowly add dry ingredients to wet ingredients, and mix on medium speed until smooth, about 1 minute.

Using a large spoon, fill the cupcake liners three-quarters full and bake for 18 to 20 minutes, or until a toothpick inserted in the center comes out clean. Let cool for 20 minutes.

ORANGE MASCARPONE FROSTING

½ cup butter, softened
2 ounces (about ¼ cup) mascarpone cheese
Zest of one orange (reserve some for garnish)
2 tablespoons chardonnay
2 cups powdered sugar

With a hand or stand mixer, beat softened butter and mascarpone cheese together on medium speed for 3 minutes.

Add orange zest and chardonnay and mix on medium speed until thoroughly combined.

Slowly add powdered sugar and beat on low for 1 minute. Gradually increase the speed to high and beat for 3 minutes, until fluffy.

To Assemble Cupcakes
Gently pipe each cupcake with Orange Mascarpone Frosting. Garnish with a sprinkle of orange zest on each cupcake.

WHITE CHOCOLATE COCONUT CUPCAKE +WHITE CHOCOLATE LIME BUTTERCREAM

This is a Cupcake Wars *winning recipe! This cupcake was inspired by the movie* White Christmas. *The coconut sprinkled on top reminds me of new fallen snow, and it perfectly complements the white chocolate. This cupcake can also easily be made gluten-free, without sacrificing any flavor. Just substitute gluten-free flour for the regular flour when called for.*

WHITE CHOCOLATE COCONUT CUPCAKE

¾ cup butter, softened

2 eggs plus 2 egg whites

1⅓ cups granulated sugar

1 teaspoon pure vanilla extract

2 teaspoons pure coconut extract

¾ cup coconut milk

1¾ cups all-purpose (or gluten-free) flour

2 teaspoons baking powder

½ teaspoon salt

1½ cups shredded sweetened coconut

1 cup white chocolate chips

Preheat the oven to 350°F. Line two standard cupcake tins with 20 paper liners.

Using a stand or hand mixer, cream together the butter, eggs, egg whites, and sugar on medium speed in a large bowl.

Reduce speed to low and add vanilla extract, coconut extract, and coconut milk.

In a separate bowl, combine flour, baking powder, and salt. Slowly add dry ingredients to wet ingredients, and mix on medium speed until smooth, about 2 minutes.

Stir in shredded coconut and white chocolate chips with a spatula.

Using a large spoon, fill the cupcake liners three-quarters full and bake for 18 to 20 minutes, or until a toothpick inserted in the center comes out clean. Let cool for 20 minutes.

WHITE CHOCOLATE LIME BUTTERCREAM

1½ cups butter, softened
Juice of 2 limes
1 cup white chocolate chips
2 cups powdered sugar
Sweetened shredded coconut, for garnish
12 lime wedges, for garnish

With a hand or stand mixer, beat softened butter and lime juice together on medium speed for 3 minutes.

In a small saucepan, heat white chocolate chips over medium heat.

Stir constantly with a wooden spoon, until they are completely melted and smooth, about 1 to 2 minutes.

Add melted white chocolate to butter mixture and beat on medium until smooth, about 3 minutes.

Slowly add powdered sugar and beat on low for 1 minute. Gradually increase the speed and beat for 3 minutes, until fluffy.

To Assemble Cupcakes
Gently pipe each cupcake with White Chocolate Lime Buttercream. Garnish with a sprinkle of sweetened shredded coconut and lime wedge, if desired.

ELDERFLOWER CUPCAKE ✛ LEMON ZEST BUTTERCREAM

I'm a sucker for anything with elderflower liqueur, usually in martinis or champagne cocktails that have a splash added in. A few years ago, I was pairing mini cupcakes with martinis at a local bar, and I decided to try creating an elderflower cupcake to pair with an elderflower martini. It was a hit. I've since discovered that this cupcake also pairs well with a semisweet or sweet sparkling wine.

ELDERFLOWER CUPCAKE

1 cup granulated sugar

¾ cup butter, softened

2 eggs

1 teaspoon pure vanilla extract

½ cup elderflower liqueur

¼ cup sour cream

¾ cup all-purpose flour

½ cup self-rising flour

½ teaspoon baking soda

¼ teaspoon salt

Preheat the oven to 350°F. Line two standard cupcake tins with 15 paper liners.

Using a stand or hand mixer, cream together the sugar and butter on medium speed in a large bowl.

Slowly add in eggs, one at a time, and mix on medium speed until combined.

Reduce speed to low and add vanilla extract, elderflower liqueur, and sour cream.

In a separate bowl, combine both flours, baking soda, and salt. Slowly add dry ingredients to wet ingredients, and mix on medium speed until smooth, about 2 minutes.

Using a large spoon, fill the cupcake liners three-quarters full and bake for 18 to 20 minutes, or until a toothpick inserted in the center comes out clean. Let cool for 20 minutes.

LEMON ZEST BUTTERCREAM

½ cup butter, softened
3 tablespoons elderflower liqueur
1 teaspoon lemon zest
3 cups powdered sugar
12 freshly cut flowers, for garnish, if desired

With a hand or stand mixer, beat softened butter on medium speed for 1 minute.

Add elderflower liqueur and lemon zest, and beat on low for 1 minute.

Slowly add powdered sugar and beat on low for another minute.

Gradually increase the speed to high and beat for 3 minutes, until fluffy.

To Assemble Cupcakes
Gently pipe each cupcake with Lemon Zest Buttercream. Garnish each cupcake with a freshly cut flower, if desired.

2
FRUITY + BERRY

30
Peach Wildflower
Honey Cupcake
+ Honey Peach
Filling
+ Honey
Mascarpone
Frosting

34
Strawberry
Shortcake Cupcake
+ Fresh Strawberry
Filling
+ Vanilla Whipped
Cream Frosting

38
Cherry Thyme
Cupcake
+ Cherry
Buttercream

43
Banana Cupcake
+ Rum Mango
Filling
+ Banana Rum
Frosting

45
Fig Cupcake
+ Pear and Fig
Filling
+ Honey Brie
Buttercream

48
Blueberry Sour
Cream Cupcake
+ Lemon Sour
Cream Frosting

52
Honey Ricotta
Cheesecake
Cupcake
+ Macerated
Balsamic
Strawberries
with Basil
Topping

56
White Chocolate
Raspberry Cupcake
+ Raspberry Cream
Frosting

PEACH WILDFLOWER HONEY CUPCAKE + HONEY PEACH FILLING + HONEY MASCARPONE FROSTING

In Santa Barbara, we have a wonderful farmer's market on Tuesday afternoons on State Street, the main street downtown. I love stopping by the San Marcos Farms' stand and picking up some local wildflower honey. Bake this cupcake when peaches are in season, and try to find some local honey, as the freshness of the ingredients will make all the difference.

PEACH WILDFLOWER HONEY CUPCAKE

1 cup granulated sugar
¾ cup butter, softened
2 eggs
1 teaspoon pure vanilla extract
¼ cup whole milk
½ cup sour cream
¾ cup all-purpose flour
½ cup self-rising flour
½ teaspoon baking soda
¼ teaspoon salt

Preheat oven to 350°F. Line two standard cupcake tins with 15 paper liners.

Using a stand or hand mixer, cream together the sugar and butter on medium speed in a large bowl.

Slowly add in eggs, one at a time, and mix on medium speed until combined.

Reduce speed to low and add vanilla extract, milk, and sour cream. In a separate bowl, combine both flours, baking soda, and salt.

Slowly add dry ingredients to wet ingredients, and mix on medium speed until smooth, about 2 minutes.

Using a large spoon, fill the cupcake liners three-quarters full and bake for 18 to 20 minutes, or until a toothpick inserted in the center comes out clean. Let cool for 20 minutes.

HONEY PEACH FILLING

2 peaches, diced into ½-inch pieces
¼ cup wildflower honey

In a small bowl, mix peaches with wildflower honey until coated well.

HONEY MASCARPONE FROSTING

½ cup butter, softened
4 ounces (about ½ cup) mascarpone cheese
2 cups powdered sugar
1 tablespoon wildflower honey
Peach slices, as garnish
Wildflower honey, as topping drizzle

With a hand or stand mixer, cream softened butter and mascarpone cheese together on medium speed for 2 minutes.

Slowly add powdered sugar and beat on low for 2 minutes.

Add honey and gradually increase the speed to high and beat for 3 minutes, until fluffy.

To Assemble Cupcakes
Using an apple corer or a circle pastry tip, poke a quarter-sized hole in each cupcake and remove a small amount of cupcake inside. Spoon a tablespoon of Honey Peach Filling into each cupcake. Gently pipe each cupcake with Honey Mascarpone Frosting. Garnish with a slice of fresh peach and a drizzle of wildflower honey.

STRAWBERRY SHORTCAKE CUPCAKE + FRESH STRAWBERRY FILLING + VANILLA WHIPPED CREAM FROSTING

For those expecting a cakey texture to this cupcake, be forewarned! This is very much shortcake in cupcake form, so the cake itself is slightly crispy and crumbly, much like a biscuit. The vanilla whipped cream adds a dose of light and airy sweetness.

STRAWBERRY SHORTCAKE CUPCAKE

¼ cup granulated sugar

⅓ cup butter, softened

¾ cup half-and-half

¼ cup orange juice

1½ cups all-purpose flour

½ cup self-rising flour

2 teaspoons baking powder

1 teaspoon salt

12 finely diced strawberries, for filling

Preheat the oven to 400°F. Line a standard cupcake tin with 12 paper liners.

Using a stand or hand mixer, cream together the sugar and butter on medium speed in a large bowl.

In a small bowl, combine half-and-half and orange juice, set aside.

In a separate bowl, combine both flours, baking powder, and salt. Slowly add the wet ingredients and the dry ingredients alternately to the butter mixture.

Mix on medium speed until smooth, about 1 minute.

Using a large spoon, fill the cupcake liners three-quarters full. Bake for 15 to 17 minutes, or until cupcakes are slightly browned around the edges.

VANILLA WHIPPED CREAM FROSTING

1 cup butter, softened
½ teaspoon pure vanilla extract
½ cup heavy whipping cream
4 cups powdered sugar
4 strawberries, cut into slices, for garnish

With a hand or stand mixer using a whisk attachment, beat softened butter on medium speed for 1 minute.

Add vanilla extract and half of the whipping cream and mix on medium speed until thoroughly combined.

Slowly add powdered sugar and beat on low for 1 minute.

Add other half of whipping cream and gradually increase the speed to high and beat for 3 minutes, until fluffy.

To Assemble Cupcakes

Using an apple corer or a circle pastry tip, poke a quarter-sized hole in each cupcake and remove a small amount of cupcake inside. Spoon a tablespoon of the finely diced strawberries into each cupcake. Gently pipe each cupcake with Vanilla Whipped Cream Frosting. Garnish with a strawberry slice on top of each cupcake.

CHERRY THYME CUPCAKE + CHERRY BUTTERCREAM

I was inspired to create this cupcake by a good friend whose birthday was coming up soon. I asked him what cupcakes he wanted me to bake for him, and he requested a cupcake with cherry and thyme, which I'd never tried before! It was perfect, because his birthday was in early June, and cherries were still in season. Depending on where you live, cherries may be in season during different months, so be sure to check.

CHERRY THYME CUPCAKE

1 cup granulated sugar
1 cup olive oil
2 eggs
1 teaspoon pure vanilla extract
¼ cup whole milk
½ cup sour cream
¾ cup all-purpose flour
½ cup self-rising flour
½ teaspoon baking soda
¼ teaspoon salt
2 teaspoons ground thyme
½ cup finely diced fresh cherries, liquid strained

Preheat the oven to 350°F. Line a standard cupcake tin with 12 paper liners.

Using a stand or hand mixer, cream together the sugar and olive oil on medium speed in a large bowl.

Slowly add in eggs, one at a time, and mix on medium speed until combined.

Reduce speed to low and add vanilla extract, milk, and sour cream.

In a separate bowl, combine both flours, baking soda, salt, and thyme. Slowly add dry ingredients to wet ingredients, and mix on medium speed until smooth, about 1 minute.

With a spatula, fold cherries into the cupcake batter.

Using a large spoon, fill the cupcake liners three-quarters full and bake for 18 to 20 minutes, or until a toothpick inserted in the center comes out clean.

CHERRY BUTTERCREAM

½ cup butter, softened
5 cherries, finely diced, liquid strained
2½ cups powdered sugar
12 cherries, for garnish
12 thyme sprigs, for garnish

With a hand or stand mixer, beat softened butter on medium speed for 1 minute.

Add cherries and beat on medium speed for 1 minute.

Slowly add powdered sugar and beat on low for 1 minute.

Gradually increase the speed to high and beat for 3 minutes, until fluffy.

To Assemble Cupcakes
Gently pipe each cupcake with Cherry Buttercream. Garnish with a fresh cherry and thyme sprig on top of each cupcake.

BANANA CUPCAKE + RUM MANGO FILLING + BANANA RUM FROSTING

I was inspired to make this cupcake from a cocktail I created on New Year's Eve one year called a "Tropical Baby Guinness." The drink had a very strange combination of rum, banana, and mango, along with some Kahlua and Baileys Irish Cream. Although the cocktail was not a winner, this cupcake is!

BANANA CUPCAKE

5 ripe bananas
(4 for cupcakes, 1 for garnish)
1 cup sugar
2 eggs
¼ cup sour cream
¾ cup olive oil
2 cups all-purpose flour
2 teaspoons baking soda
1 teaspoon baking powder

TOTAL
TIME
80
minutes

Preheat oven to 325°F. Line two standard cupcake tins with 18 paper liners.

In a medium mixing bowl, mash 4 bananas until they have the consistency of baby food.

Add sugar, eggs, and sour cream, and beat together on medium speed until smooth, about 2 minutes.

Add olive oil and beat for another 30 seconds.

In a separate bowl, mix together the flour, baking soda, and baking powder. Slowly stir in the flour mixture to the wet mixture, and beat on medium speed for 2 to 3 minutes, until thoroughly combined.

Using a large spoon, fill the cupcake liners three-quarters full and bake for 20 to 25 minutes, or until a toothpick inserted in the center comes out clean. Let cool for 20 minutes.

RUM MANGO FILLING

2 mangos (save one for garnish)
¼ cup dark Puerto Rican rum

_____

Remove skin from one mango and discard. Chop mango into small cubes and place in a blender.

Add rum and blend on high for 1 minute, or until the mixture has the consistency of smooth applesauce.

BANANA RUM FROSTING

1 cup butter, softened
¼ banana
4 cups powdered sugar
1 tablespoon dark Puerto Rican rum

_____

With a hand or stand mixer, beat softened butter and banana together on medium speed for 3 minutes.

Slowly add powdered sugar and beat on low for 1 minute.

Add rum and gradually increase the speed to high and beat for 3 minutes, until fluffy.

To Assemble Cupcakes
Using an apple corer or a circle pastry tip, poke a quarter-sized hole in each cupcake and remove a small amount of cupcake inside. Spoon a tablespoon of Rum Mango Filling into each cupcake. Gently pipe each cupcake with Banana Rum Frosting. Garnish with a slice of banana and mango on each cupcake.

FIG CUPCAKE + PEAR AND FIG FILLING + HONEY BRIE BUTTERCREAM

If you can't find fresh figs, dried figs actually work just as well in this recipe. Since the figs for the filling will be simmering over low heat for 8 to 10 minutes, they will soften up and almost melt into the cupcake as a filling.

FIG CUPCAKE

1 cup granulated sugar
1 cup olive oil
2 eggs
1 teaspoons pure vanilla extract
¼ cup whole milk
½ cup sour cream
¾ cup all-purpose flour
½ cup self-rising flour
½ teaspoon baking soda
¼ teaspoon salt
½ cup finely diced figs

TOTAL TIME
80
minutes

12
CUPCAKES

Preheat the oven to 350°F. Line a standard cupcake tin with 12 paper liners.

Using a stand or hand mixer, cream together the sugar and olive oil on medium speed in a large bowl.

Slowly add in eggs, one at a time, and mix on medium speed until combined.

Reduce speed to low and add vanilla extract, milk, and sour cream.

In a separate bowl, combine both flours, baking soda, and salt. Slowly add dry ingredients to wet ingredients, and mix on medium speed until smooth, about 2 minutes.

With a spatula, fold diced figs into the cupcake batter.

Using a large spoon, fill the cupcake liners three-quarters full and bake for 18 to 20 minutes, or until a toothpick inserted in the center comes out clean.

PEAR AND FIG FILLING

12 figs, finely diced
1 pear, finely diced
½ cup granulated sugar

In a small saucepan, combine figs, pear, and sugar over low heat for 8 to 10 min, or until pear is soft and the sugar turns to syrup.

Remove from heat and let cool.

HONEY BRIE BUTTERCREAM

½ cup butter, softened
4 ounces (about ½ cup) brie cheese, diced (with rind)
½ cup honey
2½ cups powdered sugar
6 figs, cut in half, for garnish

With a hand or stand mixer, beat softened butter and brie on medium speed for 1 minute.

Add honey and beat on medium speed for 1 minute.

Slowly add powdered sugar and beat on low for 1 minute.

Gradually increase the speed to high and beat for 3 minutes, until fluffy.

To Assemble Cupcakes
Once cool, poke small holes in each cupcake, using a circle pastry tip or an apple corer. Insert one tablespoon of the Fig and Pear Filling into each cupcake. Gently pipe each cupcake with Honey Brie Buttercream. Garnish each cupcake with a fig half.

BLUEBERRY
SOUR CREAM
CUPCAKE
— LEMON
SOUR CREAM
FROSTING

BLUEBERRY SOUR CREAM CUPCAKE

1 cup granulated sugar
½ cup butter, softened
1 egg
1 cup sour cream
¾ teaspoon pure vanilla extract
½ cup all-purpose flour
¾ cup self-rising flour
1 teaspoon baking powder
¼ teaspoon salt
½ cup fresh blueberries

TOTAL TIME
70
minutes

12 CUPCAKES

Every time I had attempted a cupcake with blueberries in the batter, they had always fallen to the bottom of the cupcake. I've learned to fill the cupcake liners with batter first, then drop the blueberries in and slightly cover them with batter. This technique keeps them from completely sinking to the bottom.

Preheat the oven to 350°F. Line a standard cupcake tin with 12 paper liners.

Using a stand or hand mixer, cream together the sugar and butter on medium speed in a large bowl.

Add in the egg and mix on medium speed until combined.

Reduce speed to low and add sour cream and vanilla extract.

In a separate bowl, combine both flours, baking powder, and salt. Slowly add dry ingredients to wet ingredients, and mix on medium speed until smooth, about 2 minutes.

Using a large spoon, fill the cupcake liners three-quarters full.

Drop 3 or 4 blueberries into each cupcake and push down slightly so that the blueberries are just covered with batter.

Bake for 30 to 35 minutes, or until edges are golden and slightly crispy.

49

LEMON SOUR CREAM FROSTING

½ cup butter, softened
1 tablespoon sour cream
3 cups powdered sugar
2 tablespoons lemon juice
12 fresh blueberries, for garnish

With a hand or stand mixer, beat softened butter for 1 minute.

Add sour cream and beat on medium speed for 1 minute.

Slowly add powdered sugar and beat on low for 1 minute.

Add lemon juice, gradually increase the speed to high, and beat for 3 minutes, until fluffy.

To Assemble Cupcakes
Gently pipe each cupcake with Lemon Sour Cream Frosting. Garnish each cupcake with a fresh blueberry.

HONEY RICOTTA CHEESECAKE CUPCAKE + MACERATED BALSAMIC STRAWBERRIES WITH BASIL TOPPING

A dessert my friend made one night when we were having a "Breakfast for Dinner" party inspired me to create this cupcake recipe. She macerated the strawberries with an amazing dark chocolate balsamic vinegar. Feel free to experiment with different flavored balsamic vinegars, a fig or lemon balsamic would work well with this cupcake.

HONEY RICOTTA CHEESECAKE CUPCAKE

6 ounces vanilla wafers, about 35–40 wafers

¼ cup butter

24 ounces cream cheese

1 cup granulated sugar

2 large eggs

½ cup ricotta cheese

¼ cup honey

Preheat the oven to 325°F. Line a standard cupcake tin with 12 paper liners.

In a blender or food processor, pulse together the vanilla wafers until they resemble fine sand. Transfer wafer crumbs to a medium bowl and set aside.

In a separate, small bowl, melt butter in the microwave until it is completely liquid.

Pour butter into the vanilla wafer crumbs and mix well with a fork, until the mixture is thoroughly combined.

Press one rounded tablespoon of the wafer mixture into the bottom of each cupcake liner.

Using a stand or hand mixer on the lowest speed, beat together the cream cheese and sugar until smooth.

Beat in one egg at a time, increasing the speed to high after the last egg is added.

Beat for about 3 minutes, until the batter is smooth. Lowering the speed to low, add the ricotta cheese and honey, and mix for 1 minute.

The cheesecake will sink slightly after baking and will provide a nice well for the strawberry topping.

Fill cupcake liners all the way to the top; they will hardly rise at all during baking.

Bake for 25 to 30 minutes, or until cheesecake starts to crack on the top, and the edges are slightly golden. Remove from oven and chill in the refrigerator for 20 minutes, or until firm. While cupcakes are chilling, prepare Macerated Balsamic Strawberries with Basil Topping.

MACERATED BALSAMIC STRAWBERRIES WITH BASIL TOPPING

3 cups strawberries (about 1½ pints), diced into ½-inch cubes
1 tablespoon balsamic vinegar
1½ tablespoons granulated sugar
Juice of ½ lemon
12 basil leaves, finely chopped
Fresh black pepper, for garnish

In a medium bowl, combine diced strawberries with balsamic vinegar, sugar, and lemon.

Mix until strawberries are thoroughly coated.

Stir in chopped basil.

To Assemble Cupcakes
Spoon 1½ tablespoons of topping onto each Honey Ricotta Cheesecake Cupcake. Grind a dash of fresh black pepper on top of each cupcake.

WHITE CHOCOLATE RASPBERRY CUPCAKE + RASPBERRY CREAM FROSTING

The white chocolate in this cupcake comes from white chocolate chips, which are chopped up finely with a chef's knife before they are incorporated into the batter. You can also pulse the chips in a food processor to get tiny pieces. This way, the white chocolate disperses more evenly into the cupcake than if it is in big chunks.

WHITE CHOCOLATE RASPBERRY CUPCAKE

1 cup granulated sugar
¾ cup butter, softened
2 eggs
2 teaspoons raspberry extract
¼ cup whole milk
½ cup sour cream
¾ cup all-purpose flour
½ cup self-rising flour
½ teaspoon baking soda
¼ teaspoon salt
1 cup white chocolate chips, chopped finely into tiny pieces

Preheat oven to 350°F. Line two standard cupcake tins with 15 paper liners.

Using a stand or hand mixer, cream together the sugar and butter on medium speed in a large bowl.

Slowly add in eggs, one at a time, and mix on medium speed until combined.

Reduce speed to low and add raspberry extract, milk, and sour cream.

In a separate bowl, combine both flours, baking soda, and salt. Slowly add dry ingredients to wet ingredients, and mix on medium speed until smooth, about 1 minute.

Using a spatula, fold in white chocolate chip pieces.

Using a large spoon, fill the cupcake liners three-quarters full and bake for 20 to 25 minutes, or until a toothpick inserted in the center comes out clean. Let cool for 20 minutes.

RASPBERRY CREAM FROSTING

1 cup butter, softened
4 ounces (about ½ cup) cream cheese
½ teaspoon raspberry extract
3 cups powdered sugar
15 fresh raspberries, for garnish
¼ cup shaved white chocolate, for garnish

With a hand or stand mixer, beat softened butter and cream cheese together on medium speed for 3 minutes.

Add raspberry extract and mix on medium speed until thoroughly combined.

Slowly add powdered sugar and beat on low for 1 minute.

Gradually increase the speed to high and beat for 3 minutes, until fluffy.

To Assemble Cupcakes

Gently pipe each cupcake with Raspberry Cream Frosting. Garnish with a fresh raspberry and a sprinkle of shaved white chocolate on top of each cupcake.

3
SALTY + NUTTY

62
Banana Cupcake
+ Caramel
Bourbon Sauce
+ Caramel
Banana Filling
+ Salted Caramel
Bourbon Frosting

66
Pistachio
Cupcake
+ Orange
Mascarpone
Frosting

68
Dark Chocolate
Cupcake
+ Salted
Chocolate
Frosting

70
Almond Cupcake
+ Cherry Rum
Filling
+ Almond Cream
Cheese Frosting

74
Chocolate
Hazelnut Cupcake
+ Nutella
Frosting

76
Pumpkin Bread
Pudding Cupcake
+ Caramel Sauce
+ Salted Caramel
Frosting

80
Chocolate
Almond Cupcake
+ Dark Chocolate
Frosting
+ Almond Butter
Frosting

BANANA CUPCAKE + CARAMEL BOURBON SAUCE + CARAMEL BANANA FILLING + SALTED CARAMEL BOURBON FROSTING

The most amazing Bananas Foster I've ever had, served at The Palace Grill, a Cajun-Creole restaurant in Santa Barbara, was the inspiration for this cupcake. The combination of warm caramel sauce, bananas, and a hint of booze is perfection. Pair this cupcake with a scoop of vanilla bean ice cream on the side to send it over the top.

BANANA CUPCAKE

1 cup granulated sugar
¾ cup butter, softened
2 eggs
1 teaspoon pure banana extract
¼ cup whole milk
½ cup sour cream
¾ cup all-purpose flour
½ cup self-rising flour
½ teaspoon baking soda
¼ teaspoon salt

Preheat oven to 350°F. Line a standard cupcake tin with 12 paper liners.

Using a stand or hand mixer, cream together the sugar and butter on medium speed in a large bowl.

Slowly add in eggs, one at a time, and mix on medium speed until combined.

Reduce speed to low and add banana extract, milk, and sour cream.

In a separate bowl, combine both flours, baking soda, and salt. Slowly add dry ingredients to wet ingredients, and mix on medium speed until smooth, about 2 minutes.

Using a large spoon, fill the cupcake liners three-quarters full and bake for 18 to 20 minutes, or until a toothpick inserted in the center comes out clean. Let cool for 20 minutes.

CARAMEL BOURBON SAUCE

¼ cup butter

2 tablespoons bourbon

¼ cup white sugar

¼ cup brown sugar

½ cup heavy cream

½ teaspoon sea salt

In a medium saucepan, slowly melt butter over low heat.

Stir in the bourbon and sugars until sugar is dissolved, about 1 minute.

Add heavy cream and salt and stir over medium heat, whisking constantly, for about 3 to 4 minutes.

Take off heat and pour into a mason jar. Put directly into the fridge to cool for 30 minutes.

CARAMEL BANANA FILLING

1 ripe banana, diced into ¼-inch pieces

¼ cup Caramel Bourbon Sauce

In a small bowl, mix bananas with ¼ cup of the Caramel Bourbon Sauce until coated well.

SALTED CARAMEL BOURBON FROSTING

½ cup butter, softened
½ cup Caramel Bourbon Sauce
3 cups powdered sugar
¼ teaspoon sea salt
12 banana slices, for garnish

With a hand or stand mixer, beat softened butter and ½ cup of the Caramel Bourbon Sauce together on medium speed for 1 minute.

Slowly add powdered sugar and beat on low for 2 minutes.

Add salt and gradually increase the speed to high and beat for 3 minutes, until fluffy.

To Assemble Cupcakes
Using an apple corer or a circle pastry tip, poke a quarter-sized hole in each cupcake and remove a small amount of cupcake inside. Spoon a tablespoon of Caramel Banana Filling into each cupcake. Gently pipe each cupcake with Salted Caramel Bourbon Frosting. Garnish with a slice of banana and drizzle of Caramel Bourbon Sauce.

PISTACHIO CUPCAKE + ORANGE MASCARPONE FROSTING

I created this cupcake for my dad, who is the pistachio king of our family. It's rare that a Christmas or birthday goes by where one of us doesn't buy him a bag of fancy pistachios. I remember one year I carried four bags of pistachios on a plane from California to New York because I found some gourmet, flavored pistachios that I knew he would love.

PISTACHIO CUPCAKE

5 ounces shelled pistachios

1 cup granulated sugar

¾ cup butter, softened

3 eggs

¼ teaspoon pure vanilla extract

½ cup whole milk

¾ cup all-purpose flour

¼ cup self-rising flour

1½ teaspoons baking powder

½ teaspoon salt

½ teaspoon cinnamon

½ teaspoon nutmeg

Preheat oven to 350°F. Line two standard cupcake tins with 16 paper liners.

With a blender or food processer, grind pistachios until they are the texture of find sand. Set aside.

Using a stand or hand mixer, cream together the sugar and butter on medium speed in a large bowl.

Slowly add in eggs, one at a time, and mix on medium speed until combined.

Reduce speed to low and add vanilla extract and milk.

In a separate bowl, combine both flours, baking powder, salt, cinnamon, and nutmeg. Slowly add dry ingredients to wet ingredients, and mix on medium speed until smooth, about 2 minutes.

Using a spatula, fold in ground pistachios.

Using a large spoon, fill the cupcake liners three-quarters full and bake for 18 to 20 minutes, or until a toothpick inserted in the center comes out clean. Let cool for 20 minutes.

ORANGE MASCARPONE FROSTING

¾ cup butter, softened
6 ounces (about ¾ cup) mascarpone cheese
4 teaspoons orange zest
3 cups powdered sugar
16 whole pistachios, for garnish

With a hand or stand mixer, beat softened butter and mascarpone cheese together on medium speed for 3 minutes.

Add orange zest and mix on medium speed until thoroughly combined.

Slowly add powdered sugar and beat on low for 1 minute.

Gradually increase the speed to high and beat for 3 minutes, until fluffy.

To Assemble Cupcakes
Gently pipe each cupcake with Orange Mascarpone Frosting. Garnish with a pistachio piece on top.

DARK CHOCOLATE CUPCAKE + SALTED CHOCOLATE FROSTING

I am obsessed with anything sweet and salty, from chocolate-covered pretzels to salted caramel ice cream. This dark chocolate cupcake hits that same spot for me; it's hard to have just one!

DARK CHOCOLATE CUPCAKE

⅓ cup olive oil
¾ cup granulated sugar
½ cup whole milk
½ cup sour cream
1½ teaspoons vanilla extract
¾ cup all-purpose flour
¼ cup self-rising flour
⅓ cup cocoa powder
1 teaspoon baking soda
½ teaspoon baking powder
½ teaspoon salt
1 cup bittersweet chocolate chips

Preheat the oven to 350°F. Line a standard cupcake tin with 12 paper liners.

Using a stand or hand mixer, cream together the oil and sugar on medium speed in a large bowl.

Reduce speed to low and add milk, sour cream, and vanilla extract.

In a separate bowl, combine flours, cocoa powder, baking soda, baking powder, and salt. Slowly add dry ingredients to wet ingredients, and mix on medium speed until smooth, about 2 minutes.

Slowly add chocolate chips and mix on medium speed for 1 minute, or until combined.

Using a large spoon, fill the cupcake liners three-quarters full and bake for 18 to 20 minutes, or until a toothpick inserted in the center comes out clean. Let cool for 20 minutes.

SALTED CHOCOLATE
FROSTING

½ cup butter, softened
2½ cups powdered sugar
¼ cup heavy whipping cream
¼ cup cocoa powder
½ teaspoon sea salt
Sea salt, for garnish

With a hand or stand mixer, beat softened butter on medium speed for 3 minutes.

Slowly add half of the powdered sugar and beat on low for 1 minute.

Add heavy whipping cream, cocoa powder, and sea salt, and beat for another minute, until combined.

Slowly add the rest of the powdered sugar and gradually increase the speed to high. Beat for 3 minutes, until fluffy.

To Assemble Cupcakes
Gently pipe each cupcake with Salted Chocolate Frosting. Garnish with a sprinkle of sea salt on each cupcake.

ALMOND CUPCAKE +CHERRY RUM FILLING +ALMOND CREAM CHEESE FROSTING

The smell of almond extract always reminds me of the first time I took a cake decorating class. The instructor insisted that we add almond extract to every frosting we made, which to me seemed like overkill. But in small doses, a little almond extract can be a wonderful addition to cake and frosting.

ALMOND CUPCAKE

1 cup granulated sugar

1 cup olive oil

2 eggs

1 teaspoon pure almond extract

¼ cup whole milk

½ cup sour cream

¾ cup all-purpose flour

½ cup self-rising flour

½ teaspoon baking soda

¼ teaspoon salt

½ cup sliced almonds

Preheat the oven to 350°F. Line a standard cupcake tin with 12 paper liners.

Using a stand or hand mixer, cream together the sugar and olive oil on medium speed in a large bowl.

Slowly add in eggs, one at a time, and mix on medium speed until combined.

Reduce speed to low and add almond extract, milk, and sour cream.

In a separate bowl, combine both flours, baking soda, and salt. Slowly add dry ingredients to wet ingredients, and mix on medium speed until smooth, about 2 minutes.

With a spatula, gently fold in sliced almonds.

Using a large spoon, fill the cupcake liners three-quarters full. Bake for 18 to 20 minutes, or until cupcakes are slightly browned around the edges.

CHERRY RUM FILLING

24 fresh pitted cherries, finely diced

⅓ cup dark rum

Place cherries in a medium bowl and pour rum over them. Let the cherries soak in the rum mixture for 30 minutes.

Using a colander, drain leftover rum from cherry mixture and discard.

ALMOND CREAM CHEESE FROSTING

½ cup butter, softened

4 ounces (about ½ cup) cream cheese

¼ teaspoon pure almond extract

2 cups powdered sugar

12 fresh cherries, for garnish

¼ cup sliced almonds, for garnish

With a hand or stand mixer, beat softened butter and cream cheese together on medium speed for 3 minutes.

Add almond extract and mix on medium speed until thoroughly combined.

Slowly add powdered sugar and beat on low for 1 minute.

Gradually increase the speed to high and beat for 3 minutes, until fluffy.

To Assemble Cupcakes

Using an apple corer or a circle pastry tip, poke a quarter-sized hole in each cupcake and remove a small amount of cupcake inside. Spoon a tablespoon of Cherry Rum Filling into each cupcake. Gently pipe each cupcake with Almond Cream Cheese Frosting. Garnish with a fresh cherry and sprinkle of sliced almonds on each cupcake.

CHOCOLATE HAZELNUT CUPCAKE + NUTELLA FROSTING

This recipe is dangerous because it means you actually have to crack open a jar of Nutella and try to see if you can keep it around the house for longer than a day or two. For me, that's usually impossible! Fair warning, this Nutella Frosting will have you wanting to eat it by the spoonful.

CHOCOLATE HAZELNUT CUPCAKE

¾ cup granulated sugar

⅓ cup olive oil

1½ teaspoons vanilla extract

½ cup whole milk

½ cup sour cream

¾ cup all-purpose flour

¼ cup self-rising flour

⅓ cup cocoa powder

1 teaspoon baking soda

¼ teaspoon salt

¼ cup Nutella

½ cup chopped hazelnuts

Preheat the oven to 350°F. Line a standard cupcake tin with 12 paper liners.

Using a stand or hand mixer, cream together the sugar and olive oil on medium speed in a large bowl.

Reduce speed to low and add vanilla extract, milk, and sour cream.

In a separate bowl, combine flours, cocoa powder, baking soda, and salt. Slowly add dry ingredients to wet ingredients, and mix on medium speed until smooth, about 2 minutes.

Add Nutella and mix on medium speed for 1 minute. Gently fold in chopped hazelnuts.

Using a large spoon, fill the cupcake liners three-quarters full and bake for 18 to 20 minutes, or until a toothpick inserted in the center comes out clean. Let cool for 20 minutes.

NUTELLA FROSTING

½ cup butter, softened

2 ounces (about ¼ cup) cream cheese

2 cups powdered sugar

½ cup Nutella

¼ cup crushed hazelnuts, for garnish

With a hand or stand mixer, beat softened butter and cream cheese on medium speed for 3 minutes. Slowly add half of the powdered sugar and beat on low for 1 minute.

Add Nutella and beat on low for 1 minute.

Slowly add the rest of the powdered sugar and gradually increase the speed to high. Beat for 3 minutes, until fluffy.

To Assemble Cupcakes

Gently pipe each cupcake with Nutella Frosting. Garnish with a teaspoon of crushed hazelnuts on each cupcake.

PUMPKIN BREAD PUDDING CUPCAKE + CARAMEL SAUCE + SALTED CARAMEL FROSTING

Although this cupcake isn't made the way bread pudding is traditionally made, it has the same soft, almost creamy texture thanks to the pumpkin and caramel. Around October and November, I can't stop baking everything and anything pumpkin related — and this cupcake is one that people keep requesting.

PUMPKIN BREAD PUDDING CUPCAKE

1 cup granulated sugar

1 cup butter, softened

2 eggs

2 egg yolks

1½ cups pureed pumpkin

2 cups self-rising flour

1 teaspoon baking powder

½ teaspoon salt

2 teaspoons pumpkin pie spice

½ teaspoon cinnamon

1 cup chopped pecans

Preheat oven to 350°F. Line two standard cupcake tins with 20 paper liners.

Using a stand or hand mixer, cream together the sugar and butter on medium speed in a large bowl.

Slowly add in eggs and egg yolks, one at a time, and mix on medium speed until combined.

Reduce speed to low and add pureed pumpkin.

In a separate bowl, combine flour, baking powder, salt, pumpkin pie spice, and cinnamon. Slowly add dry ingredients to wet ingredients, and mix on medium speed until smooth, about 2 minutes.

With a spatula, gently fold in pecan pieces.

Using a large spoon, fill the cupcake liners three-quarters full and bake for 18 to 20 minutes, or until a toothpick inserted in the center comes out clean. Let cool for 20 minutes.

CARAMEL SAUCE

½ cup butter
½ cup white sugar
½ cup brown sugar
1 cup heavy cream
1 teaspoon sea salt

In a medium saucepan, slowly melt butter over low heat.

Stir the white and brown sugar until sugar is dissolved, about 1 minute.

Add heavy cream and salt and stir over medium heat, whisking constantly, for about 3 to 4 minutes.

Take off heat and pour into a mason jar. Put directly into the fridge to cool for 30 minutes.

SALTED CARAMEL FROSTING

¾ cup butter, softened
¾ cup Caramel Sauce
4½ cups powdered sugar
½ teaspoon sea salt
¼ cup pecan pieces, for garnish

With a hand or stand mixer, beat softened butter and ¾ cup of the Caramel Sauce together on medium speed for 2 minutes.

Slowly add powdered sugar and beat on low for 2 minutes.

Add salt and gradually increase the speed to high and beat for 3 minutes, until fluffy.

To Assemble Cupcakes
Using an apple corer or a circle pastry tip, poke a quarter-sized hole in each cupcake and remove a small amount of cupcake inside. Spoon a half tablespoon of the Caramel Sauce into each cupcake. Gently pipe each cupcake with Salted Caramel Frosting. Garnish with a sprinkle of pecan pieces on each cupcake.

CHOCOLATE
ALMOND
CUPCAKE
+ DARK
CHOCOLATE
FROSTING
+ ALMOND
BUTTER
FROSTING

I remember the day I got hooked on almond butter. I was training for a half-marathon, and I didn't have any food in the house for a pre-race snack, so I stopped by a local market and bought a small container of almond butter and a package of English muffins. Not only was it a tasty treat, but I had one of the best runs ever that morning. It wasn't long after then that I created my almond butter frosting.

CHOCOLATE ALMOND CUPCAKE

⅓ cup olive oil
¾ cup granulated sugar
½ cup whole milk
½ cup sour cream
1½ teaspoons almond extract
¾ cup all-purpose flour
¼ cup self-rising flour
⅓ cup cocoa powder
1 teaspoon baking soda
½ teaspoon baking powder
½ teaspoon salt
1 cup sliced almonds

TOTAL TIME
70
minutes

12
CUPCAKES

Preheat the oven to 350°F. Line a standard cupcake tin with 12 paper liners.

Using a stand or hand mixer, cream together the oil and sugar on medium speed in a large bowl.

Reduce speed to low and add milk, sour cream, and almond extract.

In a separate bowl, combine flours, cocoa powder, baking soda, baking powder, and salt. Slowly add dry ingredients to wet ingredients, and mix on medium speed until smooth, about 2 minutes.

Slowly add sliced almonds and mix on medium speed for 1 minute, or until combined.

Using a large spoon, fill the cupcake liners three-quarters full and bake for 18 to 20 minutes, or until a toothpick inserted in the center comes out clean. Let cool for 20 minutes.

DARK CHOCOLATE FROSTING

½ cup butter, softened
2½ cups powdered sugar
¼ cup heavy whipping cream
¼ cup cocoa powder

With a hand or stand mixer, beat softened butter on medium speed for 3 minutes.

Slowly add half of the powdered sugar and beat on low for 1 minute.

Add heavy whipping cream and cocoa powder and beat for another minute, until combined.

Slowly add the rest of the powdered sugar and gradually increase the speed to high. Beat for 3 minutes, until fluffy.

ALMOND BUTTER FROSTING

¼ cup butter
1 ounce (about 2 tablespoons) cream cheese
1 cup powdered sugar
¼ cup creamy almond butter
¼ cup whole or slivered almonds, for garnish

With a hand or stand mixer, beat softened butter and cream cheese on medium speed for 3 minutes.

Slowly add half of the powdered sugar and beat on low for 1 minute.

Add almond butter and beat for another minute, until combined.

Slowly add the rest of the powdered sugar and gradually increase the speed to high. Beat for 3 minutes, until fluffy.

To Assemble Cupcakes
Gently pipe each cupcake with Dark Chocolate Frosting. On top of that, gently pipe a dollop of Almond Butter Frosting. Garnish with a sprinkle of whole or slivered almonds on each cupcake.

4
CHOCOLATE

86
Flourless
Chocolate
Cupcake
+ Chocolate
Ganache
+ Fresh Whipped
Cream

91
Black Forest
Cupcake
+ Cherry Crème
de Cacao Filling
+ Chocolate
Cherry Frosting

94
Chocolate Pinot
Noir Cupcake
+ Strawberry
Compote Filling
+ Dark Chocolate
Frosting

98
Chocolate
Blackberry
Mojito Cupcake
+ Rum Lime
Buttercream

100
Cookies 'n' Cream
Cupcake
+ Classic Cream
Cheese Frosting

102
Chocolate
Malt Cupcake
+ Toasted
Marshmallow
Meringue

105
Chocolate
Raspberry
Cupcake
+ Triple Berry
Compote Filling
+ Dark Chocolate
Frosting

109
Red Wine Velvet
Cupcake
+ Classic Cream
Cheese Frosting

112
Chocolate Black
Bean Cupcake
+ Lime Ricotta
Frosting

FLOURLESS CHOCOLATE CUPCAKE + CHOCOLATE GANACHE + FRESH WHIPPED CREAM

FLOURLESS CHOCOLATE CUPCAKE

½ cup whole milk

½ teaspoon salt

1 cup granulated sugar

20 ounces bittersweet chocolate

1½ cups butter, softened

3 teaspoons vanilla extract

¼ cup cocoa powder

5 eggs, 1 egg yolk

This is a cupcake that is completely gluten-free, without even trying! Rich and fudgy, this reminds me of my Granny's "fudge pie" that she would make when I visited her in Denver. Topped with a dark chocolate ganache, chocoholics will love this cupcake.

Preheat the oven to 350°F. Line two standard cupcake tins with 18 paper liners.

In a small saucepan over low heat, combine the milk, salt, and sugar. Stir until salt and sugar are completely dissolved, about 3 minutes. Set aside.

Melt bittersweet chocolate in the microwave at high heat, stirring after every minute. It should take 3 to 4 minutes to become completely smooth.

Pour the melted chocolate into the bowl of an electric mixer.

Cut the butter into pieces, and beat the butter into the chocolate at medium speed, until combined, about 1 minute.

Beat in the warm milk mixture on low speed, for 30 seconds.

Add vanilla extract and cocoa powder and combine for 30 seconds, on low speed.

Slowly beat in the eggs and egg yolk, one at a time.

Using a large spoon, fill the cupcake liners three-quarters full and bake for 25 minutes, or until a toothpick inserted in the center comes out clean. Let cool for 20 minutes.

CHOCOLATE GANACHE

10 ounces bittersweet chocolate chips
1 cup heavy cream
¼ teaspoon salt

In a double boiler, heat chocolate and cream together until smooth and creamy, about 5 minutes.

Stir in salt with a wooden spoon and remove from heat.

Let sit for 5 minutes before assembling cupcakes.

FRESH WHIPPED CREAM

1½ cups heavy whipping cream
4 tablespoons granulated sugar
¼ teaspoon vanilla extract

Combine cream, granulated sugar, and vanilla extract in a mixing bowl.

Using a stand mixer, beat on high for 3 to 4 minutes, or until the cream begins to form peaks. Do not overbeat, as the cream can start to become lumpy in texture.

To Assemble Cupcakes

Gently spread a tablespoon of
Chocolate Ganache on top of each
cupcake. Spoon a generous dollop
of Fresh Whipped Cream on top.
Garnish with a drizzle of leftover
Chocolate Ganache, if desired.

BLACK FOREST CUPCAKE + CHERRY CRÈME DE CACAO FILLING + CHOCOLATE CHERRY FROSTING

This chocolate cupcake, and many of the other chocolate cupcakes in this cookbook, contains no eggs. I adapted this recipe from a vegan chocolate cupcake recipe, and I just love the flavor and texture of the cake.

BLACK FOREST CUPCAKE

¾ cup granulated sugar

⅓ cup olive oil

1½ teaspoons vanilla extract

½ cup whole milk

½ cup sour cream

¾ cup all-purpose flour

¼ cup self-rising flour

⅓ cup cocoa powder

1 teaspoon baking soda

¼ teaspoon salt

TOTAL TIME

60

minutes

12 CUPCAKES

Preheat the oven to 350°F. Line a standard cupcake tin with 12 paper liners.

Using a stand or hand mixer, cream together the sugar and olive oil on medium speed in a large bowl.

Reduce speed to low and add vanilla extract, milk, and sour cream.

In a separate bowl, combine flours, cocoa powder, baking soda, and salt. Slowly add dry ingredients to wet ingredients, and mix on medium speed until smooth, about 2 minutes.

Using a large spoon, fill the cupcake liners three-quarters full and bake for 18 to 20 minutes, or until a toothpick inserted in the center comes out clean. Let cool for 20 minutes.

CHERRY CRÈME DE CACAO FILLING

1 (21-ounce) can cherry pie filling
½ cup crème de cacao

——————

Remove 4 tablespoons of cherry pie syrup from the can of cherry pie filling and set aside for the Chocolate Cherry Frosting.

Heat 2 cups cherry pie filling and crème de cacao over medium-high heat.

Stir constantly with a wooden spoon for 5 minutes.

Remove from heat. Let cool.

CHOCOLATE CHERRY FROSTING

1 cup butter, softened
4 tablespoons cherry pie syrup
¼ cup cocoa powder
4 cups powdered sugar

——————

With a hand or stand mixer, beat softened butter on medium speed for 1 minute.

Add cherry pie syrup and cocoa powder and beat on low for 1 minute.

Slowly add the powdered sugar and gradually increase the speed to high. Beat for 3 minutes, until fluffy.

To Assemble Cupcakes
Using an apple corer or a circle pastry tip, poke a quarter-sized hole in each cupcake and remove a small amount of cupcake inside. Spoon a tablespoon of Cherry Crème de Cacao Filling into each cupcake. Gently pipe each cupcake with Chocolate Cherry Frosting. Garnish with a dollop of leftover Cherry Crème de Cacao Filling on top of each cupcake.

CHOCOLATE PINOT NOIR CUPCAKE +STRAWBERRY COMPOTE FILLING +DARK CHOCOLATE FROSTING

This cupcake can be made with almost any berry of your choice substituted for the strawberries. One of my friends has a severe allergy to strawberries, so she substitutes raspberries for the strawberries, and it works just as beautifully.

CHOCOLATE PINOT NOIR CUPCAKE

2 cups granulated sugar

1 cup unsalted butter, softened

4 eggs

1 teaspoon vanilla extract

1½ cups pinot noir

2 cups all-purpose flour

½ cup self-rising flour

1½ cups cocoa powder

1 teaspoon baking soda

1 teaspoon salt

Preheat the oven to 350°F. Line two standard cupcake tins with 20 paper liners.

Using a stand or hand mixer, cream together the sugar and butter on medium speed in a large bowl.

Slowly add in eggs, one at a time, and mix on medium speed until combined.

Reduce speed to low and add vanilla extract and pinot noir.

In a separate bowl, combine flours, cocoa powder, baking soda, and salt. Slowly add dry ingredients to wet ingredients, and mix on medium speed until smooth, about 2 minutes.

Using a large spoon, fill the cupcake liners three-quarters full and bake for 18 to 20 minutes, or until a toothpick inserted in the center comes out clean. Let cool for 20 minutes. While cupcakes are cooling, start Strawberry Compote Filling.

STRAWBERRY COMPOTE FILLING

16 ounces fresh strawberries,
diced into 1-inch pieces
(about 2 cups after diced)
½ cup pinot noir
½ cup sugar

In a medium saucepan, heat strawberries, pinot noir, and sugar over medium heat, stirring until sugar is dissolved.

Once sugar is dissolved, bring heat up to high and bring mixture to a boil.

Boil for 5 minutes, then reduce heat to low and simmer for 10 minutes, stirring every 2 minutes.

Strawberry mixture should be reduced by half and slightly thickened. Remove from heat and let cool.

DARK CHOCOLATE FROSTING

½ cup butter, softened
2 cups powdered sugar
½ cup heavy whipping cream
½ cup cocoa powder

With a hand or stand mixer, beat softened butter on medium speed for 3 minutes. Slowly add half of the powdered sugar and beat on low for 1 minute.

Add heavy whipping cream and beat on low for 1 minute.

Slowly add the cocoa powder and the rest of the powdered sugar and gradually increase the speed to high. Beat for 3 minutes, until fluffy.

To Assemble Cupcakes

Once cool, poke small holes in each cupcake, using a circle pastry tip or an apple corer. Insert one tablespoon of the Strawberry Compote Filling into each cupcake. Gently pipe each cupcake with Dark Chocolate Frosting. Garnish with a heaping spoonful of Strawberry Compote Filling on top.

CHOCOLATE BLACKBERRY MOJITO CUPCAKE + RUM LIME BUTTERCREAM

My brother-in-law is known for making the world's best mojitos, and this recipe is my spin on his classic cocktail. Refreshing, rich, and a little tart, this cupcake reminds me of sitting outside on my family's deck in Vermont, mojito in hand.

CHOCOLATE BLACKBERRY MOJITO CUPCAKE

2 eggs
1 cup granulated sugar
2 teaspoons vanilla extract
1 cup sour cream
1 cup all-purpose flour
⅓ cup cocoa powder
¾ teaspoon baking soda
½ teaspoon baking powder
¼ teaspoon salt
⅓ cup olive oil
24 blackberries

Preheat the oven to 350°F. Line a standard cupcake tin with 12 paper liners.

Using a stand or hand mixer, cream together the eggs and sugar on medium speed in a large bowl.

Reduce speed to low and add vanilla extract and sour cream.

In a separate bowl, combine flour, cocoa powder, baking soda, baking powder, and salt. Slowly add dry ingredients to wet ingredients, and mix on medium speed until smooth, about 2 minutes.

Slowly add olive oil and mix on medium speed for 1 minute, or until combined.

Using a large spoon, fill the cupcake liners three-quarters full and bake for 18 to 20 minutes, or until a toothpick inserted in the center comes out clean. Let cool for 20 minutes.

RUM LIME BUTTERCREAM

¾ cup butter, softened

3 cups powdered sugar

1 tablespoon lime juice

2 tablespoons dark rum

12 sprigs fresh mint, for garnish

With a hand or stand mixer, beat softened butter on medium speed for 3 minutes. Slowly add half of the powdered sugar and beat on low for 1 minute.

Add lime juice and rum, and beat on low for 1 minute.

Slowly add the rest of the powdered sugar and gradually increase the speed to high. Beat for 3 minutes, until fluffy.

To Assemble Cupcakes

Once cool, poke small holes in each cupcake, using a circle pastry tip or an apple corer. Insert one blackberry into each cupcake. Gently pipe each cupcake with Rum Lime Buttercream. Garnish with a blackberry and fresh mint sprig on each cupcake.

COOKIES 'N' CREAM CUPCAKE + CLASSIC CREAM CHEESE FROSTING

While growing up, my favorite part of an Oreo was the vanilla cream center. I think that's why I love frosting so much — it tastes like a childhood treat. This cupcake brings me back to those days; scraping out the center of an Oreo and saving it for last.

COOKIES 'N' CREAM CUPCAKE

1 cup granulated sugar
¾ cup butter, softened
2 eggs
3 teaspoons pure vanilla extract
¼ cup whole milk
½ cup sour cream
¾ cup all-purpose flour
½ cup self-rising flour
½ teaspoon baking soda
¼ teaspoon salt
1 cup smashed up Oreo cookies

Preheat oven to 350°F. Line two standard cupcake tins with 15 paper liners.

Using a stand or hand mixer, cream together the sugar and butter on medium speed in a large bowl.

Slowly add in eggs, one at a time, and mix on medium speed until combined.

Reduce speed to low and add vanilla extract, milk, and sour cream.

In a separate bowl, combine both flours, baking soda, and salt. Slowly add dry ingredients to wet ingredients, and mix on medium speed until smooth, about 2 minutes.

Using a spatula, fold in smashed up Oreo cookies.

Using a large spoon, fill the cupcake liners three-quarters full and bake for 18 to 20 minutes, or until a toothpick inserted in the center comes out clean. Let cool for 20 minutes.

CLASSIC CREAM CHEESE FROSTING

½ cup butter, softened
4 ounces (about ¼ cup) cream cheese
¼ teaspoon pure vanilla extract
2 cups powdered sugar
8 Oreos, cut in half

With a hand or stand mixer, beat softened butter and cream cheese together on medium speed for 3 minutes.

Add vanilla extract and mix on medium speed until thoroughly combined.

Slowly add powdered sugar and beat on low for 1 minute.

Gradually increase the speed to high and beat for 3 minutes, until fluffy.

To Assemble Cupcakes
Gently pipe each cupcake with Classic Cream Cheese Frosting. Garnish with an Oreo cookie piece on top.

CHOCOLATE MALT CUPCAKE + TOASTED MARSHMALLOW MERINGUE

This cupcake is one of my Cupcake Wars winning cupcakes! I based this cupcake after the classic movie A Christmas Story. *It's inspired by the scene where Ralphie receives his secret decoder ring, only to find out the secret message from Orphan Annie was, "Be sure to drink your Ovaltine." With the toasted marshmallow meringue frosting, eating this cupcake is like enjoying a piping mug of hot chocolate.*

CHOCOLATE MALT CUPCAKE

½ cup flour
1½ cups powdered sugar
3 eggs
1 teaspoon vanilla
⅔ cup Ovaltine (or other chocolate malt mix)
6 ounces bittersweet chocolate
2 ounces semisweet chocolate
½ cup plus 2 tablespoons butter

TOTAL TIME
60
minutes

15
CUPCAKES

Preheat oven to 400°F. Line two standard cupcake tins with 15 paper liners.

In a medium-sized mixing bowl, combine flour, powdered sugar, eggs, vanilla, and Ovaltine. Set aside.

In a double boiler over medium heat, melt the chocolates and butter, stirring constantly.

When the mixture is creamy and everything has melted (about 5 to 8 minutes), remove from heat and fold into the flour mixture with a spatula.

Once the two mixtures are thoroughly combined, fill cupcake liners to three-quarters full and bake for 15 to 18 minutes. The edges should be firm but the center should be slightly creamy. To check the doneness, insert a toothpick in the center. It should not come out clean, but the cupcakes will be firm around the edges, not jiggly to the touch.

TOASTED MARSHMALLOW
MERINGUE

4 egg whites

1 cup sugar

⅛ teaspoon cream of tarter

Combine egg whites, sugar, and
cream of tartar in metal mixing bowl.
Place over a double boiler and whisk
until the sugar is dissolved.

Keep whisking constantly, until a
candy thermometer inserted into the
mixture reaches 145°F.

Immediately remove from heat and
beat on the highest speed with a
hand or stand mixer for about 10 to 15
minutes, or until firm peaks form.

To Assemble Cupcakes

Gently pipe each cupcake with
Toasted Marshmallow Meringue.
Using a chef's torch, lightly toast the
tops of the meringue by holding the
torch about 4 to 6 inches away from
the top of the cupcake. It should be
lightly golden, or darker, depending
on how toasty you want the frosting
to be.

CHOCOLATE RASPBERRY CUPCAKE + TRIPLE BERRY COMPOTE FILLING + DARK CHOCOLATE FROSTING

When my sister and I were kids, our mom would stuff our Christmas stockings with all sorts of goodies, including raspberry jelly candies that were covered in chocolate. I loved them so much that I would savor them so they'd last throughout the holiday season. Now, the combination of chocolate and raspberry brings back that nostalgia of those chocolate-covered raspberry candies.

CHOCOLATE RASPBERRY CUPCAKE

¾ cup granulated sugar
⅓ cup olive oil
½ teaspoon vanilla extract
½ teaspoon raspberry extract
1 cup whole milk
¾ cup all-purpose flour
¼ cup self-rising flour
⅓ cup cocoa powder
1 teaspoon baking soda
¼ teaspoon salt
½ cup mini chocolate chips

TOTAL TIME
90
minutes

Preheat the oven to 350°F. Line a standard cupcake tin with 12 paper liners.

Using a stand or hand mixer, cream together the sugar and olive oil on medium speed in a large bowl.

Reduce speed to low and add vanilla extract, raspberry extract, and milk.

In a separate bowl, combine flours, cocoa powder, baking soda, and salt. Slowly add dry ingredients to wet ingredients, and mix on medium speed until smooth, about 2 minutes.

With a spatula, gently fold in mini chocolate chips.

Using a large spoon, fill the cupcake liners three-quarters full and bake for 18 to 20 minutes, or until a toothpick inserted in the center comes out clean. Let cool for 20 minutes. While cupcakes are cooling, start Triple Berry Compote Filling.

TRIPLE BERRY COMPOTE FILLING

½ cup blueberries
½ cup raspberries
½ cup blackberries
½ cup sugar
Juice of ½ lemon

In a medium saucepan, heat berries, sugar, and lemon over medium heat. Gently mash the berries with a wooden spoon to break them apart and release their juices.

Once sugar is dissolved, reduce heat to low and simmer for 2 minutes.

Remove from heat and let cool.

DARK CHOCOLATE FROSTING

½ cup butter, softened
2 cups powdered sugar
½ cup heavy whipping cream
½ cup cocoa powder

With a hand or stand mixer, beat softened butter on medium speed for 3 minutes. Slowly add half of the powdered sugar and beat on low for 1 minute.

Add heavy whipping cream and beat on low for 1 minute.

Slowly add the cocoa powder and the rest of the powdered sugar and gradually increase the speed to high. Beat for 3 minutes, until fluffy.

To Assemble Cupcakes
Using an apple corer or a circle
pastry tip, poke a quarter-sized hole
in each cupcake and remove a small
amount of cupcake inside. Insert
one tablespoon of the Triple Berry
Compote Filling into each cupcake.
Gently pipe each cupcake with Dark
Chocolate Frosting. Garnish with
a heaping spoonful of Triple Berry
Compote Filling on top.

RED WINE
VELVET
CUPCAKE
+ CLASSIC
CREAM CHEESE
FROSTING

Julia Child is quoted as saying,
"I enjoy cooking with wine,
sometimes I even put it
in the food I'm cooking."
That explains this cupcake.
The addition of red wine gives
this chocolate-based cupcake
a more complex depth of
flavor, as well as a boozy
kick. Feel free to bake these
cupcakes with a glass of red
wine in hand!

RED WINE VELVET CUPCAKE

1 cup granulated sugar
½ cup butter, softened
2 eggs
½ teaspoon pure vanilla extract
½ cup dry red wine, such as cabernet sauvignon
½ tablespoon red food coloring
1 cup all-purpose flour
¼ cup self-rising flour
½ teaspoon baking soda
½ teaspoon salt
¼ cup cocoa powder

TOTAL
TIME
50
minutes

Preheat the oven to 350°F. Line a standard cupcake tin with 12 paper liners.

Using a stand or hand mixer, cream together the sugar and butter on medium speed in a large bowl.

Slowly add in eggs, one at a time, and mix on medium speed until combined.

Reduce speed to low and add vanilla extract, red wine, and food coloring.

In a separate bowl, combine both flours, baking soda, salt, and cocoa powder. Slowly add dry ingredients to wet ingredients, and mix on medium speed until smooth, about 2 minutes.

Using a large spoon, fill the cupcake liners three-quarters full and bake for 18 to 20 minutes, or until a toothpick inserted in the center comes out clean. Let cool for 20 minutes.

CLASSIC CREAM CHEESE FROSTING

½ cup butter, softened
4 ounces (about ½ cup) cream cheese
¼ teaspoon pure vanilla extract
2 cups powdered sugar

With a hand or stand mixer, beat softened butter and cream cheese together on medium speed for 3 minutes.

Add vanilla and mix on medium speed until thoroughly combined.

Slowly add powdered sugar and beat on low for 1 minute. Gradually increase the speed to high and beat for 3 minutes, until fluffy.

To Assemble Cupcakes
Gently pipe each cupcake with Classic Cream Cheese Frosting.

CHOCOLATE BLACK BEAN CUPCAKE + LIME RICOTTA FROSTING

A few years ago I was dared to try baking a "burrito" cupcake. I added black beans to the chocolate batter, and served it in a crispy tortilla. It definitely didn't taste like a burrito, but the black bean flavor came through and gave the chocolate cake a moist texture. Thus, the black bean cupcake was born!

CHOCOLATE BLACK BEAN CUPCAKE

¾ cup granulated sugar
⅓ cup olive oil
½ cup whole milk
½ cup sour cream
1 teaspoon vanilla extract
¾ cup all-purpose flour
½ cup self-rising flour
1 teaspoon baking soda
½ cup cocoa powder
½ teaspoon salt
1 (15-ounce) can black beans, drained, rinsed, and mashed

Preheat the oven to 350°F. Line a standard cupcake tin with 12 paper liners.

Using a stand or hand mixer, cream together the sugar and olive oil on medium speed in a large bowl.

Slowly add in milk, sour cream, and vanilla extract and mix on low speed until combined.

In a separate bowl, combine both flours, baking soda, cocoa powder, and salt. Slowly add dry ingredients to wet ingredients, and mix on medium speed until smooth, about 2 minutes.

Reduce speed to low and add black beans, mix for 2 minutes.

Using a large spoon, fill the cupcake liners three-quarters full and bake for 18 to 20 minutes, or until a toothpick inserted in the center comes out clean.

LIME RICOTTA FROSTING

½ cup butter, softened
½ tablespoon lime juice
¼ cup ricotta cheese
3 cups powdered sugar
¼ cup black beans for garnish, if desired

With a hand or stand mixer, beat softened butter for 1 minute.

Add lime juice and ricotta cheese, and beat on medium speed for 1 minute.

Slowly add powdered sugar and beat on low for 1 minute.

Gradually increase the speed to high and beat for 3 minutes, until fluffy.

To Assemble Cupcakes
Gently pipe each cupcake with Lime Ricotta Frosting. Sprinkle each cupcake with a few black beans for garnish, if desired.

5

SPICE +
CINNAMON +
MAPLE +
COFFEE

116
Classic
 Carrot Cake
+ Cinnamon
Cream Cheese
Frosting

118
Maple Cupcake
+ Maple
Buttercream
+ Crispy Bacon
Topping

122
Mulled Wine
Cupcake
+ Cinnamon
Brandy Frosting
+ Candied Orange
Peel Topping

126
Chocolate Chai
Cupcake with
Chai Tea
Infused Milk
+ Chai Spiced
Buttercream

131
Tiramisu
Cupcake
+ Coffee Liqueur
Mascarpone
Frosting

134
Cinnamon
Apple Cupcake
+ Cinnamon
Apple Filling
+ Cinnamon
Cream Cheese
Frosting
+ Apple Fritter
Topping

138
Chocolate Chip
Waffle Cupcake
+ Maple Cream
Cheese Frosting
+ Buttermilk
Waffle Topping

CLASSIC CARROT CAKE + CINNAMON CREAM CHEESE FROSTING

This is a super moist cake with a rich, cinnamon flavor. I'm more of a carrot cake purist myself; I'm not a huge fan of raisins or nuts in carrot cake. However, you could certainly add some into this recipe if desired.

CLASSIC CARROT CAKE

1 cup granulated sugar

2 eggs

½ cup olive oil

½ teaspoon pure vanilla extract

1 cup all-purpose flour

1 teaspoon baking soda

½ teaspoon salt

1½ teaspoons ground cinnamon

1½ cups finely grated carrots

Preheat the oven to 350°F. Line a standard cupcake tin with 12 paper liners.

Using a stand or hand mixer, cream together the sugar and eggs on medium speed in a large bowl.

Add in olive oil and vanilla and mix on medium speed until combined.

In a separate bowl, combine flour, baking soda, salt, and cinnamon.

Slowly add dry ingredients to wet ingredients, and mix on medium speed until smooth, about 2 minutes.

With a spatula, fold in grated carrots until all ingredients are combined.

Using a large spoon, fill the cupcake liners three-quarters full and bake for 18 to 20 minutes, or until a toothpick inserted in the center comes out clean. Let cool for 20 minutes.

CINNAMON CREAM CHEESE FROSTING

½ cup butter, softened

4 ounces cream cheese

¼ teaspoon pure vanilla extract

2 cups powdered sugar

1½ teaspoons cinnamon

¼ cup grated carrot, for garnish (if desired)

With a hand or stand mixer, beat softened butter and cream cheese together on medium speed for 3 minutes.

Add vanilla and mix on medium speed until thoroughly combined.

Slowly add powdered sugar and beat on low for 1 minute.

Add cinnamon and gradually increase the speed to high and beat for 3 minutes, until fluffy.

To Assemble Cupcakes

Gently pipe each cupcake with Cinnamon Cream Cheese Frosting. Garnish each cupcake with a sprinkle of grated carrot, if desired.

MAPLE CUPCAKE + MAPLE BUTTERCREAM + CRISPY BACON TOPPING

I baked these cupcakes for a bacon-themed party a few years ago, and they were an absolute hit! I'd like to think they stood out against all the other bacon delights, such as bacon wrapped hot dogs, bacon guacamole, and bacon mac 'n' cheese. Just make sure the bacon is nice and crispy for that sweet and salty crunch.

MAPLE CUPCAKE

1 cup granulated sugar

¾ cup butter, softened

2 eggs

1 teaspoon pure vanilla extract

4 teaspoons pure maple extract

¼ cup whole milk

½ cup sour cream

¾ cup all-purpose flour

½ cup self-rising flour

½ teaspoon baking soda

¼ teaspoon salt

¼ cup pure maple syrup

Preheat the oven to 350°F. Line two standard cupcake tins with 15 paper liners.

Using a stand or hand mixer, cream together the sugar and butter on medium speed in a large bowl.

Slowly add in eggs, one at a time, and mix on medium speed until combined.

Reduce speed to low and add both extracts, milk, and sour cream.

In a separate bowl, combine both flours, baking soda, and salt. Slowly add dry ingredients to wet ingredients, and mix on medium speed until smooth, about 1 minute.

Using a large spoon, fill the cupcake liners three-quarters full and bake for 18 to 20 minutes, or until a toothpick inserted in the center comes out clean. As soon as the cupcakes come out, poke holes in the top of each cupcake while hot with a fork. Soak each cupcake with 1 teaspoon pure maple syrup. Let cool for 20 minutes.

MAPLE BUTTERCREAM

¾ cup butter, softened
¼ cup pure maple syrup
½ teaspoon pure maple extract
3 cups powdered sugar

With a hand or stand mixer, beat softened butter, maple syrup, and maple extract together on medium speed for 3 minutes.

Slowly add powdered sugar and beat on low for 1 minute.

Gradually increase the speed to high and beat for 3 minutes, until fluffy.

CRISPY BACON TOPPING

5 strips bacon

Preheat oven to 400°F.

Line a baking sheet with parchment paper. Place bacon strips close together (but not overlapping) on paper, and put baking sheet in oven.

Halfway through (about 10 minutes) take out the baking sheet and turn over each piece of bacon carefully with a fork.

Return to oven and bake until crispy, about 10 more minutes.

Remove from oven and carefully place each strip of bacon on a plate lined with paper towels to absorb the excess grease.

When cooled, cut each strip of bacon into thirds.

To Assemble Cupcakes

Gently pipe each cupcake with Maple Buttercream. Garnish each cupcake with a piece of crispy bacon.

MULLED WINE CUPCAKE +CINNAMON BRANDY FROSTING +CANDIED ORANGE PEEL TOPPING

This is another one of my Cupcake Wars winning recipes! I based this cupcake on the movie It's a Wonderful Life. *Clarence, the angel, mentions that his favorite drink is mulled wine, and this spiced, orangey cupcake packs a boozy punch that I'd like to think Clarence would enjoy.*

MULLED WINE CUPCAKE

2 cups all-purpose flour

1½ teaspoons baking powder

½ teaspoon baking soda

1 teaspoon ground cinnamon

1 teaspoon ground cloves

¾ cup butter, softened

⅔ cup granulated sugar

Zest of 1 orange

2 eggs

¼ cup whole milk

¼ cup dry red wine

(like cabernet sauvignon or merlot)

Mulled Wine Syrup, see recipe

Preheat the oven to 350°F. Line two standard cupcake tins with 15 paper liners.

In a large bowl, whisk together flour, baking powder, baking soda, cinnamon, and cloves. Set aside.

Using a hand or stand mixer on the lowest speed, beat butter, sugar, and grated orange zest in a large bowl for 2 minutes, until light and fluffy.

One at a time, add in the eggs. Add milk, wine, and Mulled Wine Syrup and beat for 1 minute on medium speed.

Slowly add dry ingredients, and mix on lowest speed until batter is smooth, about 2 minutes.

Using a large spoon, fill the cupcake liners three-quarters full and bake for 20 to 22 minutes, or until a toothpick inserted in the center comes out clean. Let cool for 20 minutes.

Make the Mulled Wine Syrup first, and then start on the cupcakes.

MULLED WINE SYRUP

1½ cups dry red wine

1 cup granulated sugar

4 whole cloves

1 cinnamon stick

1 orange, sliced

In a medium saucepan, heat red wine and sugar over medium-high heat until sugar is completely dissolved, stirring constantly.

Add whole cloves, cinnamon stick, and orange slices, and bring to a boil. Boil for 25 minutes, or until liquid has reduced to about 1 cup of liquid.

Strain liquid through a colander with a large bowl underneath to remove the sliced oranges, cloves, and cinnamon stick. Set aside to cool.

CINNAMON BRANDY FROSTING

1 cup butter, softened

4 ounces cream cheese

2 cups powdered sugar

2½ teaspoons cinnamon

1½ tablespoons brandy

With a hand or stand mixer, beat softened butter and cream cheese together on medium speed for 3 minutes.

Slowly add powdered sugar and beat on low for 1 minute. Gradually increase the speed and beat for 3 minutes, until fluffy.

Decrease speed to low and slowly beat in cinnamon and brandy until combined, about 1 minute.

CANDIED ORANGE PEEL

2 oranges
1 cup granulated sugar plus ½ cup for coating
1 cup water

Using a sharp paring knife, carefully cut away the peel on each orange.

Cut the peels into 15 six-inch strips, one for each cupcake.

Add 1 cup sugar and 1 cup water to a small saucepan and heat over medium-high heat, stirring with a wooden spoon until sugar is dissolved.

Add the orange peels and bring the water to a boil over high heat for 10 minutes, or until peels have softened.

Strain the peels through a colander with a large bowl underneath.

Add remaining ½ cup sugar to a separate small bowl, and toss the orange peels in the bowl until thoroughly coated with sugar.

To Assemble Cupcakes

Gently pipe each cupcake with Cinnamon Brandy Frosting. Garnish with a candied orange peel.

CHOCOLATE CHAI CUPCAKE WITH CHAI TEA INFUSED MILK + CHAI SPICED BUTTERCREAM

My sister, Catherine, used to be in love with chai lattes, and she got me hooked on them a while back. I could never have chai tea on its own, but somehow with sugar and milk it was the perfect treat. This cupcake has both sugar and milk, so it's no wonder I love it so much.

CHOCOLATE CHAI CUPCAKE

¾ cup granulated sugar

⅓ cup olive oil

1½ teaspoons pure vanilla extract

½ cup Chai Tea Infused Milk, see recipe

½ cup sour cream

¾ cup all-purpose flour

¼ cup self-rising flour

⅓ cup cocoa powder

1 teaspoon baking soda

½ teaspoon baking powder

½ teaspoon salt

Preheat the oven to 350°F. Line a standard cupcake tin with 12 paper liners.

Using a stand or hand mixer, cream together the sugar and olive oil on medium speed in a large bowl.

Reduce speed to low and add vanilla extract, Chai Tea Infused Milk, and sour cream.

In a separate bowl, combine both flours, cocoa powder, baking soda, baking powder, and salt. Slowly add dry ingredients to wet ingredients, and mix on medium speed until smooth, about 2 minutes.

Using a large spoon, fill the cupcake liners three-quarters full and bake for 18 to 20 minutes, or until a toothpick inserted in the center comes out clean. Let cool for 20 minutes.

* Make the Chai Tea Infused Milk first, and then make the cupcakes.

CHAI TEA INFUSED MILK

5 bags chai tea
1 cup whole milk

Heat tea bags and milk over high heat for 2 minutes, or until bubbles form.

Reduce to low and let simmer for 3 minutes, stirring constantly with a wooden spoon. Remove from heat and let stand for 15 minutes.

With your hands, squeeze the excess liquid from the tea bags and discard them. Save ½ cup for Chocolate Chai Cupcake batter and ¼ cup for Chai Spiced Buttercream.

CHAI SPICED BUTTERCREAM

1 cup butter, softened
¼ cup Chai Tea Infused Milk
⅛ teaspoon ginger
⅛ teaspoon cloves
3 cups powdered sugar

With a hand or stand mixer, beat softened butter on medium speed for 3 minutes.

Add Chai Tea Infused Milk and mix on medium speed until thoroughly combined.

Slowly add ginger, cloves, and powdered sugar and beat on low for 1 minute.

Gradually increase the speed to high and beat for 3 minutes, until fluffy.

To Assemble Cupcakes
Gently pipe each cupcake with Chai Spiced Buttercream.

TIRAMISU CUPCAKE + COFFEE LIQUEUR MASCARPONE FROSTING

This is the perfect "coffee" cake. I came up with this recipe a few years ago when Sugar Cat Studio in Santa Barbara was asked to bake cupcakes for a winery that was launching their new Italian varietal and wanted to have Italian-themed refreshments. Soaked with coffee liqueur, this cupcake is luscious and boozy.

TIRAMISU CUPCAKE

1 cup granulated sugar

¾ cup butter, softened

2 eggs

2 teaspoons pure vanilla extract

½ cup cold coffee

¼ cup sour cream

¾ cup all-purpose flour

½ cup self-rising flour

½ teaspoon baking soda

¼ teaspoon salt

½ cup coffee liqueur, for soaking cupcakes

TOTAL TIME

60 minutes

15 CUPCAKES

Preheat the oven to 350°F. Line two standard cupcake tins with 15 paper liners.

Using a stand or hand mixer, cream together the sugar and butter on medium speed in a large bowl.

Slowly add in eggs, one at a time, and mix on medium speed until combined.

Reduce speed to low and add vanilla extract, coffee, and sour cream.

In a separate bowl, combine both flours, baking soda, and salt. Slowly add dry ingredients to wet ingredients, and mix on medium speed until smooth, about 2 minutes.

Using a large spoon, fill the cupcake liners three-quarters full and bake for 18 to 20 minutes, or until a toothpick inserted in the center comes out clean.

When cupcakes come out of the oven and are still warm, poke holes in each cupcake with a fork. Slowly soak each cupcake with 2 teaspoons of coffee liqueur. Let cool.

COFFEE LIQUEUR MASCARPONE FROSTING

½ cup butter, softened
2 ounces mascarpone cheese
2 tablespoons coffee liqueur
3 cups powdered sugar
Dusting of cocoa powder, for garnish

With a hand or stand mixer, beat softened butter and mascarpone cheese together on medium speed for 3 minutes.

Add coffee liqueur and mix on medium speed until thoroughly combined.

Slowly add powdered sugar and beat on low for 1 minute.

Gradually increase the speed to high and beat for 3 minutes, until fluffy.

To Assemble Cupcakes
Gently pipe each cupcake with Coffee Liqueur Mascarpone Frosting. Garnish with a dusting of cocoa powder on each cupcake.

CINNAMON
APPLE CUPCAKE
+CINNAMON
APPLE FILLING
+CINNAMON
CREAM CHEESE
FROSTING
+APPLE FRITTER
TOPPING

While growing up in upstate New York, it was a tradition to go apple-picking every fall. Our local apple orchard, Beak and Skiff, sold amazing apple fritters, among other treats, such as cider donuts, caramel apples, and apple pie. These cupcakes remind me of the crisp October air and colored leaves crunching underneath my feet.

CINNAMON APPLE CUPCAKE

1 cup granulated sugar

¾ cup butter, softened

2 eggs

2 teaspoons pure vanilla extract

½ cup whole milk

¼ cup sour cream

¾ cup all-purpose flour

½ cup self-rising flour

½ teaspoon baking soda

¼ teaspoon salt

2 tablespoons cinnamon

TOTAL TIME

60

minutes

15

CUPCAKES

Preheat the oven to 350°F. Line two standard cupcake tins with 15 paper liners.

Using a stand or hand mixer, cream together the sugar and butter on medium speed in a large bowl.

Slowly add in eggs, one at a time, and mix on medium speed until combined.

Reduce speed to low and add vanilla extract, milk, and sour cream.

In a separate bowl, combine both flours, baking soda, salt, and cinnamon. Slowly add dry ingredients to wet ingredients, and mix on medium speed until smooth, about 2 minutes.

Using a large spoon, fill the cupcake liners three-quarters full and bake for 18 to 20 minutes, or until a toothpick inserted in the center comes out clean.

CINNAMON APPLE FILLING

1 apple, diced finely
¼ cup granulated sugar
½ tablespoon cinnamon

In a small saucepan over low heat, combine diced apple with sugar and cinnamon.

Simmer for 15 minutes, stirring occasionally, until apples are soft.

Set aside to fill cupcakes with later.

CINNAMON CREAM CHEESE FROSTING

½ cup butter, softened
4 ounces (about ½ cup) cream cheese
½ teaspoon pure vanilla extract
2 cups powdered sugar
2 teaspoons cinnamon

With a hand or stand mixer, beat softened butter and cream cheese together on medium speed for 3 minutes.

Add vanilla and mix on medium speed until thoroughly combined.

Slowly add powdered sugar and beat on low for 1 minute.

Add cinnamon and gradually increase the speed to high and beat for 3 minutes, until fluffy.

APPLE FRITTER TOPPING

¾ cup all-purpose flour

2 tablespoons white sugar

1 teaspoon baking powder

½ teaspoon salt

⅓ cup buttermilk

1 egg

½ tablespoon vegetable oil

1½ apples, chopped

2 cups vegetable oil, for frying

Cinnamon and sugar, for garnish

Combine flour and next seven ingredients including apples in a medium bowl.

Heat the 2 cups vegetable oil in a frying pan over medium high heat for 3 minutes. Lower heat to medium, and using an ice cream scoop or large spoon, drop ¼ cupfuls of batter into the hot oil.

Fry about 2 to 3 minutes on each side, until golden. Remove fritters with a slotted spoon, and place on a plate lined with a paper towel to absorb the excess oil.

Continue until all the batter is gone, being careful not to overcrowd the pan while frying.

While hot, sprinkle the fritters with cinnamon and sugar.

After cooled, cut fritters into pieces to top cupcakes.

To Assemble Cupcakes

Once cool, poke small holes in each cupcake, using a circle pastry tip or an apple corer. Insert one tablespoon of the Cinnamon Apple Filling into each cupcake. Gently pipe each cupcake with Cinnamon Cream Cheese Frosting. Garnish with an Apple Fritter Topping piece on top of each cupcake.

CHOCOLATE CHIP WAFFLE CUPCAKE + MAPLE CREAM CHEESE FROSTING + BUTTERMILK WAFFLE TOPPING

This cupcake is like having brunch for dessert! I grew up spending a week in Vermont every summer, and nothing beats pure Vermont maple syrup on top of chocolate chip waffles. I love to top these cupcakes with a drizzle of syrup, preferably from Vermont.

CHOCOLATE CHIP WAFFLE CUPCAKE

1 cup granulated sugar

¾ cup butter, softened

2 eggs

1 teaspoons pure vanilla extract

2 teaspoons pure maple extract

¼ cup whole milk

½ cup sour cream

¾ cup all-purpose flour

½ cup self-rising flour

½ teaspoon baking soda

¼ teaspoon salt

1 cup mini chocolate chips

Preheat oven to 350°F. Line two standard cupcake tins with 15 paper liners.

Using a stand or hand mixer, cream together the sugar and butter on medium speed in a large bowl.

Slowly add in eggs, one at a time, and mix on medium speed until combined.

Reduce speed to low and add vanilla extract, maple extract, milk, and sour cream.

In a separate bowl, combine both flours, baking soda, and salt. Slowly add dry ingredients to wet ingredients, and mix on medium speed until smooth, about 2 minutes.

Using a spatula, fold in mini chocolate chips.

Using a large spoon, fill the cupcake liners three-quarters full and bake for 18 to 20 minutes, or until a toothpick inserted in the center comes out clean. Let cool for 20 minutes.

MAPLE CREAM CHEESE FROSTING

½ cup butter, softened
4 ounces (about ½ cup) cream cheese
½ teaspoon pure maple extract
2 cups powdered sugar
2 tablespoons pure maple syrup

With a hand or stand mixer, beat softened butter and cream cheese together on medium speed for 3 minutes.

Add maple extract and beat on medium speed for another minute.

Slowly add powdered sugar and beat on low for 1 minute.

Add maple syrup and gradually increase the speed to high and beat for 3 minutes, until fluffy.

BUTTERMILK WAFFLE TOPPING

1 tablespoon granulated sugar
¼ cup vegetable oil
1 egg
1 cup buttermilk
1 teaspoon pure vanilla extract
1 cup flour
2 teaspoons baking powder
½ teaspoon salt
⅔ cup mini chocolate chips
Cooking spray

Preheat waffle iron on medium heat.

Using a stand or hand mixer, cream together the sugar and oil on medium speed in a large bowl.

Add in egg and mix on medium speed until combined.

Reduce speed to low and add buttermilk and vanilla extract.

In a separate bowl, combine flour, baking powder, and salt. Slowly add dry ingredients to wet ingredients, and mix on medium speed until smooth, about 2 minutes.

Using a spatula, fold in mini chocolate chips.

Spray waffle iron with cooking spray.

Spoon ⅓ cupful of waffle batter into waffle iron and let cook for 5 to 8 minutes, checking every 3 minutes. Waffle will be done when it's slightly golden and pulls off the iron easily.

Spray waffle iron with cooking spray before making each waffle and repeat until all the batter is gone.

Cut waffles into 2-inch by 2-inch pieces.

To Assemble Cupcakes

Gently pipe each cupcake with Maple Cream Cheese Frosting. Garnish with a Buttermilk Waffle Topping piece on top of each cupcake. If desired, drizzle cupcakes with pure maple syrup.

6
SAVORY

SHARP CHEDDAR
CUPCAKE
+ HONEY BLUE
CHEESE FROSTING
+ CANDIED PECAN
AND CHEDDAR
CRISP TOPPINGS

This cupcake was the all-star on *Cupcake Wars*. You could say this was the "winning cupcake." A personal high in my life was when Florian Bellanger tried this cupcake and said, "This is what *Cupcake Wars* is all about." This cupcake was inspired by the classic cheese plate. In my family, we always had cheese plates around the holidays. They were composed of a few types of cheeses, some nuts, and a little honey for drizzling. I tried to merge all those flavors into this cupcake.

SHARP CHEDDAR CUPCAKE

1½ cups all-purpose flour
1 cup granulated sugar
1½ teaspoons baking powder
¾ cup whole milk
¼ cup butter, softened
½ teaspoon vanilla extract
1 egg, beaten
12 ounces (about 2½ cups) extra sharp cheddar cheese, finely grated

TOTAL TIME
70
minutes

16 CUPCAKES

Preheat the oven to 350°F. Line two standard cupcake tins with 16 paper liners.

In a large bowl, whisk together flour, sugar, and baking powder.

Using a hand or stand mixer on the lowest speed, beat in the milk, butter, vanilla, and egg.

Add the grated cheese and stir with a spatula to combine.

Using a large spoon, fill the cupcake liners three-quarters full and bake for 20 to 25 minutes, or until a toothpick inserted in the center comes out clean. Let cool for 20 minutes.

HONEY BLUE CHEESE FROSTING

1 cup butter, softened
¼ cup blue cheese, crumbled
4 ounces (about ½ cup) cream cheese
3 cups powdered sugar
2 tablespoons honey

With a hand or stand mixer, beat softened butter, blue cheese, and cream cheese together on medium speed for 3 minutes.

Slowly add powdered sugar and beat on low for 1 minute.

Gradually increase the speed until you reach the highest speed, and beat for 3 minutes, until fluffy.

Decrease speed to low and slowly beat in honey until combined, about 1 minute.

CANDIED PECAN TOPPING

1½ cups pecans, finely chopped
16 whole pecans (for garnish)
½ cup plus 1 tablespoon brown sugar
1½ tablespoons softened butter
¼ cup water

Preheat oven to 400°F.

Spread all of the pecans, including the whole pecans, evenly on a 9 × 12 baking sheet. Bake for about 5 minutes to toast, and remove to cool.

Combine brown sugar, butter, and water in a medium saucepan.

Heat over medium heat until butter melts, about 4 minutes. Stir in toasted pecans.

Continue cooking over medium heat until sugar reaches full boil, stirring occasionally — watch carefully as sugar will boil fairly quickly.

As soon as mixture reaches full boil, remove from heat and transfer to a medium bowl to cool.

With a spoon, remove the whole pecans and save for garnish. When the mixture cools enough so that it is not runny, spoon candied pecans over cupcakes.

CHEDDAR CRISP TOPPING

1 cup cheddar cheese, shredded

Preheat oven to 400°F.

Line a baking sheet with parchment paper. Drop quarter-sized mounds of cheddar cheese on the sheet and bake for 5 minutes, or until cheese has melted and hardened.

Let cool for 5 minutes and gently peel off parchment paper.

To Assemble Cupcakes

Spoon a tablespoon of Candied Pecans on each cooled cupcake. Gently pipe each cupcake with Honey Blue Cheese Frosting. Finally, garnish with a Cheddar Crisp and one whole candied pecan.

ASIAGO BASIL CUPCAKE + BASIL MASCARPONE FROSTING + FRESH BASIL

For this cupcake, grating the fresh asiago cheese on a microplane would be the best choice. If you don't have one, grate the cheese on the finest section of your cheese grater, or even give it a couple pulses in your food processor or blender.

ASIAGO BASIL CUPCAKE

1½ cups all-purpose flour

1 cup granulated sugar

1½ teaspoons baking powder

¾ cup whole milk

⅓ cup butter, softened

½ teaspoon vanilla extract

1 egg, beaten

12 ounces (about 2½ cups) fresh asiago cheese, very finely grated on a microplane

6 large basil leaves, finely chopped

Preheat the oven to 350°F. Line two standard cupcake tins with 16 paper liners.

In a large bowl, whisk together flour, sugar, and baking powder.

Using a hand or stand mixer on the lowest speed, beat in the milk, butter, vanilla, and egg.

Add the grated asiago and basil, and stir with a spatula to combine.

Using a large spoon, fill the cupcake liners three-quarters full and bake for 20 to 25 minutes, or until a toothpick inserted in the center comes out clean. Let cool for 20 minutes

BASIL MASCARPONE FROSTING

¾ cup butter, softened

4 ounces (about ½ cup) mascarpone cheese

2 cups powdered sugar

5 large basil leaves, finely chopped

16 basil leaves, for garnish

With a hand or stand mixer, beat butter and mascarpone cheese together on medium speed for 3 minutes.

Slowly add powdered sugar and beat on low for 1 minute.

Add chopped basil and gradually increase the speed until you reach the highest speed, and beat for 3 minutes, until fluffy.

To Assemble Cupcakes

Gently pipe each cupcake with Basil Mascarpone Frosting. Garnish each cupcake with a fresh basil leaf.

CHICKEN 'N' WAFFLE CUPCAKE + MAPLE BUTTERCREAM + BUTTERMILK WAFFLE + CRISPY FRIED CHICKEN TOPPINGS

At first I thought the idea of fried chicken, waffles, and maple syrup was a strange combination, but I was hooked the first time I tried it. To me it's the ultimate brunch food: sweet, savory, and crunchy. This is easily one of my most popular Sunday morning cupcake flavors.

CHICKEN 'N' WAFFLE CUPCAKE

1 cup granulated sugar
¾ cup butter, softened
2 eggs
1 teaspoon pure vanilla extract
2 teaspoons pure maple extract
¼ cup whole milk
½ cup sour cream
¾ cup all-purpose flour
½ cup self-rising flour
½ teaspoon baking soda
¼ teaspoon salt
1 cup mini chocolate chips

Preheat oven to 350°F. Line two standard cupcake tins with 15 paper liners.

Using a stand or hand mixer, cream together the sugar and butter on medium speed in a large bowl.

Slowly add in eggs, one at a time, and mix on medium speed until combined.

Reduce speed to low and add vanilla extract, maple extract, milk, and sour cream.

In a separate bowl, combine both flours, baking soda, and salt. Slowly add dry ingredients to wet ingredients, and mix on medium speed until smooth, about 2 minutes.

Using a spatula, fold in mini chocolate chips.

Using a large spoon, fill the cupcake liners three-quarters full and bake for 18 to 20 minutes, or until a toothpick inserted in the center comes out clean. Let cool for 20 minutes.

* The waffles and fried chicken should be made ahead of the maple buttercream, so that they have time to cool.

BUTTERMILK WAFFLES

1 tablespoon granulated sugar
¼ cup vegetable oil
1 egg
1 cup buttermilk
1 teaspoon pure vanilla extract
1 cup flour
2 teaspoons baking powder
½ teaspoon salt
Cooking spray

Preheat waffle iron on medium heat.

Using a stand or hand mixer, cream together the sugar and oil on medium speed in a large bowl.

Add in egg and mix on medium speed until combined.

Reduce speed to low and add buttermilk and vanilla extract.

In a separate bowl, combine flour, baking powder, and salt. Slowly add dry ingredients to wet ingredients, and mix on medium speed until smooth, about 2 minutes.

Spray waffle iron with cooking spray.

Spoon ⅓ cupfuls of waffle batter into waffle iron, and let cook for 5 to 8 minutes, checking every 3 minutes. Waffle will be done when slightly golden and it pulls off the iron easily.

Spray waffle iron with cooking spray before making each waffle.

Cut waffles into 2-inch by 2-inch pieces.

CRISPY FRIED CHICKEN

½ pound boneless, skinless chicken breasts
¾ cup buttermilk
1 cup all-purpose flour
½ teaspoon cayenne pepper
2 teaspoons salt
1 teaspoon fresh ground black pepper
2 cups vegetable oil

Using a sharp knife, cut chicken breasts into 1-inch by 3-inch strips.

Pour buttermilk into a medium-sized bowl and set aside.

In a separate medium-sized bowl, combine flour, cayenne pepper, salt, and black pepper.

Dredge each chicken strip in buttermilk, then dredge in flour mixture, coating each strip completely. Set coated strips on a baking sheet and leave for 15 minutes. Flour should become paste-like on the chicken.

In a large skillet, heat oil on medium-high heat. Let oil heat up for 4 to 5 minutes.

Line a large plate with paper towels and set aside to place chicken strips on when they are done cooking.

Gently drop chicken strips in hot oil, and cook for 2 to 3 minutes on each side. Strips should be browned and crispy.

With a metal slotted spoon or spatula, remove each strip and place on the plate lined with paper towels to cool.

Cut chicken strips into 15 pieces.

MAPLE BUTTERCREAM
¾ cup butter, softened
¼ cup pure maple syrup
½ teaspoon pure maple extract
3 cups powdered sugar

With a hand or stand mixer, beat softened butter, maple syrup, and maple extract together on medium speed for 3 minutes.

Slowly add powdered sugar and beat on low for 1 minute.

Gradually increase the speed to high and beat for 3 minutes, until fluffy.

To Assemble Cupcakes
Gently pipe each cupcake with Maple Buttercream. Garnish with a Buttermilk Waffle piece and Crispy Fried Chicken piece on top of each cupcake. If desired, drizzle cupcakes with pure maple syrup.

CUCUMBER MINT CUPCAKE +CUCUMBER MINT BUTTERCREAM

As commonplace as they are, I find there is something utterly luxurious about cucumbers. On hot summer days, I'll fill up a pitcher of cold water and add fresh cucumber slices. With the addition of mint, this cupcake is refreshing and the perfect way to relax and treat yourself.

CUCUMBER MINT CUPCAKE

1 medium cucumber, seeds removed and chopped into 1-inch pieces
24 fresh mint leaves
1 tablespoon lime juice
¾ cup granulated sugar
⅔ cup butter, softened
2 eggs
1¼ cups self-rising flour
½ teaspoon salt

TOTAL TIME
60
minutes

Preheat the oven to 350°F. Line a standard cupcake tin with 12 paper liners.

Using a blender or food processor, blend together the cucumber, fresh mint, and lime juice until the mixture resembles a puree. Set aside, some will be saved for frosting.

Using a stand or hand mixer, cream together the sugar and butter on medium speed in a large bowl. Slowly add the eggs, one at a time.

Reduce speed to low and add ½ cup of the cucumber mint puree and beat for 30 seconds, until just combined.

Slowly add the flour and salt to the wet ingredients, and mix on medium speed until smooth, about 2 minutes.

Using a large spoon, fill the cupcake liners three-quarters full and bake for 18 to 20 minutes, or until a toothpick inserted in the center comes out clean. Let cool for 20 minutes.

CUCUMBER MINT BUTTERCREAM

½ cup butter
¼ cup cucumber mint puree
2 cups powdered sugar
12 mint leaves, for garnish

With a hand or stand mixer, beat softened butter on medium speed for 1 minute.

Slowly add the cucumber mint puree and the powdered sugar alternately.

Beat on low for 1 minute, then gradually increase the speed to high and beat for 3 minutes, until fluffy.

To Assemble Cupcakes
Gently pipe each cupcake with Cucumber Mint Buttercream. Garnish with a fresh mint leaf on each cupcake.

LAVENDER POLENTA CUPCAKE + LAVENDER FROSTING

I love this recipe because it gives me an excuse to whip up a big batch of polenta, and save some for dinners and lunches throughout the week. If you don't have the time to cook your own polenta, you can buy some precooked at retailers such as Trader Joe's.

LAVENDER POLENTA CUPCAKE

1 cup granulated sugar
¾ cup olive oil
3 eggs
¾ cup whole milk
½ teaspoon pure vanilla extract
1 cup all-purpose flour
½ cup self-rising flour
1 cup precooked polenta
1½ teaspoons baking powder
1 teaspoon salt

TOTAL TIME
60
minutes

12
CUPCAKES

Preheat the oven to 350°F. Line a standard cupcake tin with 12 paper liners.

Using a stand or hand mixer, cream together the sugar and olive oil on medium speed in a large bowl.

Slowly add in eggs, one at a time, and mix on medium speed until combined.

Reduce speed to low and add milk and vanilla extract.

In a separate bowl, combine both flours, polenta, baking powder, and salt. Slowly add dry ingredients to wet ingredients, and mix on medium speed until smooth, about 2 minutes.

Using a large spoon, fill the cupcake liners three-quarters full and bake for 18 to 20 minutes, or until a toothpick inserted in the center comes out clean.

LAVENDER FROSTING

½ cup butter, softened
2 ounces (about ¼ cup) cream cheese
1 tablespoon finely ground fresh lavender
2 cups powdered sugar
12 lavender sprigs, for garnish

With a hand or stand mixer, beat softened butter and cream cheese for 1 minute.

Add ground lavender and beat on medium speed for 1 minute.

Slowly add powdered sugar and beat on low for 1 minute.

Gradually increase the speed to high and beat for 3 minutes, until fluffy.

To Assemble Cupcakes
Gently pipe each cupcake with Lavender Frosting. Garnish each cupcake with a lavender sprig.

JALAPEÑO CORNBREAD CUPCAKE + HONEY BUTTER FROSTING

Sweet and spicy, this cupcake is perfect served at a barbeque. The cake is mostly savory, almost muffin-like, but the Honey Butter Frosting will remind you that, yes, this is indeed a cupcake. You could serve this as dessert, or even as a side dish with ribs, pulled pork, or brisket.

JALAPEÑO CORNBREAD CUPCAKE

⅓ cup granulated sugar

½ cup butter, softened

2 eggs

1 egg yolk

1 cup reduced-fat cultured buttermilk

¾ cup all-purpose flour

¼ cup self-rising flour

1 cup cornmeal

½ teaspoon baking soda

¾ teaspoon salt

2 jalapeños, finely diced, with seeds

Preheat the oven to 375°F. Line a standard cupcake tin with 12 paper liners.

Using a stand or hand mixer, cream together the sugar and butter on medium speed in a large bowl.

Slowly add in eggs and egg yolk, one at a time, and mix on medium speed until combined.

Reduce speed to low and add buttermilk.

In a separate bowl, combine both flours, cornmeal, baking soda, and salt. Slowly add dry ingredients to wet ingredients, and mix on medium speed until smooth, about 2 minutes.

With a spatula, fold diced jalapeños into the cupcake batter.

Using a large spoon, fill the cupcake liners three-quarters full and bake for 18 to 20 minutes, or until a toothpick inserted in the center comes out clean.

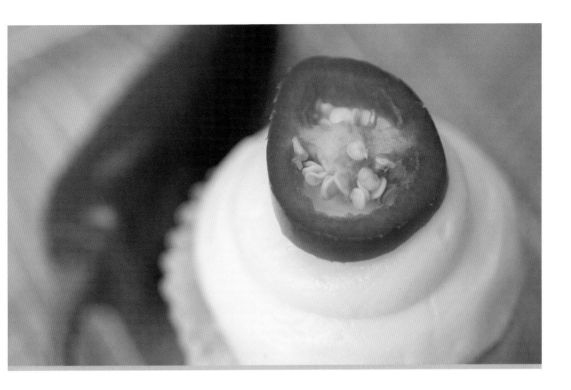

HONEY BUTTER FROSTING

1 cup butter, softened

¼ cup honey

3 cups powdered sugar

12 jalapeño slices, for garnish

With a hand or stand mixer, beat softened butter for 1 minute.

Add honey and beat on medium speed for 1 minute.

Slowly add powdered sugar and beat on low for 1 minute.

Gradually increase the speed to high and beat for 3 minutes, until fluffy.

To Assemble Cupcakes

Gently pipe each cupcake with Honey Butter Frosting. Garnish each cupcake with a slice of jalapeño.

AVOCADO CUPCAKE + SOUR CREAM LIME FROSTING

Carpinteria, a quaint little beach town outside of Santa Barbara, hosts their Avocado Festival every year in early October. They serve avocado beer, avocado ice cream, and lots of fresh guacamole. This year, I decided to give an avocado cupcake a try. I think it could only be better with some avocado ice cream on the side!

AVOCADO CUPCAKE

1 cup granulated sugar

¾ cup butter, softened

2 eggs

2 teaspoons lime juice

2 ripe avocados, mashed until smooth

2 cups self-rising flour

1 teaspoon baking powder

½ teaspoon salt

Preheat the oven to 350°F. Line two standard cupcake tins with 16 paper liners.

Using a stand or hand mixer, cream together the sugar and butter on medium speed in a large bowl.

Slowly add in eggs, one at a time, and mix on medium speed until combined.

Reduce speed to low and add lime juice and mashed avocados.

In a separate bowl, combine flour, baking powder, and salt. Slowly add dry ingredients to wet ingredients, and mix on medium speed until smooth, about 1 minute.

Using a large spoon, fill the cupcake liners three-quarters full and bake for 18 to 20 minutes, or until a toothpick inserted in the center comes out clean.

SOUR CREAM LIME FROSTING

¾ cup butter, softened

¼ cup sour cream

1 teaspoon lime juice, plus some to toss with avocados

Zest of ½ lime

2 cups powdered sugar

16 slices of avocado (tossed in lime juice to prevent browning), for garnish

With a hand or stand mixer, beat softened butter for 1 minute.

Add sour cream, lime juice, and lime zest and beat on medium speed for 1 minute.

Slowly add powdered sugar and beat on low for 1 minute.

Gradually increase the speed to high and beat for 3 minutes, until fluffy.

To Assemble Cupcakes

Gently pipe each cupcake with Sour Cream Lime Frosting. Garnish each cupcake with an avocado slice.

BUFFALO
CHICKEN
CUPCAKE
+ BLUE CHEESE
FROSTING
+ BUFFALO
CHICKEN
TOPPING

This is the perfect game day cupcake. I call these "Super Bowl Cupcakes," because I don't think I've ever been to a Super Bowl party where there wasn't a giant platter of Buffalo wings with blue cheese dressing. This cupcake is like an appetizer and dessert in one bite; it will definitely impress any sports fan.

BUFFALO CHICKEN CUPCAKE

⅓ cup granulated sugar

½ cup butter, softened

2 eggs

1 egg yolk

1 cup reduced fat cultured buttermilk

¾ cup all-purpose flour

¼ cup self-rising flour

1 cup cornmeal

½ teaspoon baking soda

¾ teaspoon salt

¼ cup honey

TOTAL TIME

90 minutes

12 CUPCAKES

Preheat the oven to 375°F. Line a standard cupcake tin with 12 paper liners.

Using a stand or hand mixer, cream together the sugar and butter on medium speed in a large bowl.

Slowly add in eggs and egg yolk, one at a time, and mix on medium speed until combined.

Reduce speed to low and add buttermilk.

In a separate bowl, combine both flours, cornmeal, baking soda, and salt. Slowly add dry ingredients to wet ingredients, and mix on medium speed until smooth, about 2 minutes.

Using a large spoon, fill the cupcake liners three-quarters full and bake for 18 to 20 minutes, or until a toothpick inserted in the center comes out clean.

When cupcakes come out of the oven and are still warm, poke holes in each cupcake with a fork. Slowly soak each cupcake with 1 teaspoon of honey. Let cool.

BLUE CHEESE FROSTING

1 cup butter, softened
¼ cup blue cheese, crumbled
4 ounces cream cheese
3 cups powdered sugar

With a hand or stand mixer, beat softened butter, blue cheese, and cream cheese together on medium speed for 3 minutes.

Slowly add powdered sugar and beat on low for 1 minute.

Gradually increase the speed until you reach the highest speed, and beat for 3 minutes, until fluffy.

BUFFALO CHICKEN TOPPING

½ pound boneless, skinless chicken breasts
¾ cup buttermilk
1 cup all-purpose flour
½ teaspoon cayenne pepper
2 teaspoons salt
1 teaspoon fresh ground black pepper
2 cups vegetable oil
¼ cup buffalo wing sauce

Using a sharp knife, cut chicken breasts into 1-inch by 3-inch strips.

Pour buttermilk into a medium-sized bowl and set aside.

In a separate medium-sized bowl, combine flour, cayenne pepper, salt, and black pepper.

Dredge each chicken strip in buttermilk, then dredge in flour mixture, coating each strip completely. Set coated strips on a baking sheet and leave for 15 minutes. Flour should become paste-like on the chicken.

In a large skillet, heat oil on medium-high heat. Let oil heat up for 4 to 5 minutes.

Line a large plate with paper towels and set aside to place chicken strips on when they are done cooking.

Gently drop chicken strips in hot oil, and cook for 2 to 3 minutes on each side. Strips should be browned and crispy.

With a metal slotted spoon or spatula, remove each strip and place on the plate lined with paper towels to cool.

Cut chicken strips into 12 pieces. In a small bowl, combine buffalo wing sauce with chicken strips and coat thoroughly.

To Assemble Cupcakes
Gently pipe each cupcake with Blue Cheese Frosting. Garnish with a piece of Buffalo Chicken on each cupcake.

ROSEMARY PARMESAN CUPCAKE + LEMON ZEST FROSTING

Rosemary has to be one of my favorite herbs to use in cooking and baking. Rosemary crackers, rosemary chicken, rosemary garlic pizza, I can't get enough. That's why I couldn't help but wonder, what about a rosemary cupcake? Add parmesan, and well, it's simply addictive. The fresh lemon frosting adds a tart sweetness to this savory cupcake.

ROSEMARY PARMESAN CUPCAKE

1½ cups all-purpose flour
1 cup granulated sugar
1½ teaspoons baking powder
¾ cup whole milk
¼ cup butter, softened
½ teaspoon vanilla extract
1 egg, beaten
12 ounces (about 2½ cups) fresh parmesan cheese, very finely grated on a microplane
2 tablespoons finely chopped fresh rosemary
16 rosemary sprigs, for garnish

Preheat the oven to 350°F. Line two standard cupcake tins with 16 paper liners.

In a large bowl, whisk together flour, sugar, and baking powder.

Using a hand or stand mixer on the lowest speed, beat in the milk, butter, vanilla, and egg.

Add the grated cheese and chopped rosemary, and stir with a spatula to combine.

Using a large spoon, fill the cupcake liners three-quarters full and bake for 20 to 25 minutes, or until a toothpick inserted in the center comes out clean. Let cool for 20 minutes

LEMON ZEST FROSTING

1 cup butter
4 ounces cream cheese
3 cups powdered sugar
Zest of 2 lemons (about 3 tablespoons)

With a hand or stand mixer, beat
softened butter and cream cheese
together on medium speed for
3 minutes.

Slowly add powdered sugar and beat
on low for 1 minute.

Add lemon zest and gradually
increase the speed until you reach
the highest speed, and beat for
3 minutes, until fluffy.

To Assemble Cupcakes
Gently pipe each cupcake with
Lemon Zest Frosting. Garnish each
cupcake with a rosemary sprig.

TOTAL
TIME
60
minutes

12
CUPCAKES

CAMEMBERT CUPCAKE + CAMEMBERT BUTTERCREAM

Camembert is my favorite cheese, so I had to try baking a cupcake with it. I have to admit I had to experiment a few times to get this one right. The trick is pushing the camembert into the cupcake batter right before it's baked, making sure it's completely covered. That prevents the camembert from bubbling up and burning.

CAMEMBERT CUPCAKE

1 cup granulated sugar
1 cup olive oil
2 eggs
1 teaspoon pure vanilla extract
¼ cup whole milk
½ cup sour cream
¾ cup all-purpose flour
½ cup self-rising flour
½ teaspoon baking soda
¼ teaspoon salt
½ tablespoon herbes de Provence
12 ounces camembert, cut into 1-ounce slices

Preheat the oven to 350°F. Line a standard cupcake tin with 12 paper liners.

Using a stand or hand mixer, cream together the sugar and olive oil on medium speed in a large bowl.

Slowly add in eggs, one at a time, and mix on medium speed until combined.

Reduce speed to low and add vanilla extract, milk, and sour cream.

In a separate bowl, combine both flours, baking soda, salt, and herbes de Provence. Slowly add dry ingredients to wet ingredients, and mix on medium speed until smooth, about 2 minutes.

Using a large spoon, fill the cupcake liners halfway full.

Add 1 ounce of sliced camembert on top of each cupcake and gently push into batter, making sure the camembert slice is covered in batter.

Bake for 18 to 20 minutes, or until cupcakes are slightly browned around the edges.

CAMEMBERT
BUTTERCREAM

½ cup butter, softened
2 ounces camembert, diced, with rind
2 cups powdered sugar
Herbes de Provence, for garnish

With a hand or stand mixer, beat
softened butter and camembert on
medium speed for 1 minute.

Slowly add powdered sugar and beat
on low for 1 minute.

Gradually increase the speed to high
and beat for 3 minutes, until fluffy.

To Assemble Cupcakes
Gently pipe each cupcake with
Camembert Buttercream. Garnish
each cupcake with a sprinkle of
herbes de Provence.

ACKNOWLEDGMENTS

I want to express my deep gratitude to those incredible people who have helped me along the way of creating this cookbook. A special thanks goes to Molly Hauge of Molly + Co (mollyandco.com), whose photography I'm constantly amazed by. I could not have found anyone who could better capture my vision for this book. Thank you to Heather Hagen of The Lion's Den (shopthelionsden.com), who provided the unique and sophisticated vintage kitchenware featured in most photos. To Emily See, thank you for your expert cupcake styling, and for being the perfect domestic curator you are. Thank you to Sherry Hopkins, who generously donated her lovely house in Carpinteria to be taken over by cupcakes, frosting, and kitchenware for two long days of photo shoots. Thank you to all my friends and family who recipe tested for me and gave me helpful advice and invaluable reviews.

I also want to thank Corks n' Crowns in Santa Barbara for opening up your tasting room to the idea of pairing cupcakes with sparkling wine, and for your constant support of Sugar Cat Studio. Thank you Florian Bellanger, for your mentorship and willingness to help in any way you could. To Erica Lively, thank you for being the best friend anyone could ever have, and for supporting Sugar Cat Studio since the beginning. I'll never forget the Christmas you bought me the domain name, sugarcatstudio.com. I can't express how grateful I am that you agreed to be my partner in crime on *Cupcake Wars*, and I would not be where I am today without you, in so many ways.

Thank you to my sister Cat and my brother-in-law Thanos, for trying each and every baking creation, especially those that were a little weird and not that pretty. Cat, I remember mailing you a "care package" of cupcakes, but they arrived all melted and smashed up, yet you still ate them! To Brian, thank you for your constant encouragement, honest feedback, and for being my personal KitchenAid mixer mechanic. Also, thank you for always tasting my baking attempts even though you happen to lack a sweet tooth.

Finally, thank you to my parents, Paul Riede and Gail Hoffman, for listening to all of my crazy ideas throughout the years. You are both amazing examples of doing what makes you happy and following your dreams, and you have always encouraged me to do the same. I'm not stopping anytime soon!

INDEX